History Of The National Flag Of The United States Of America

by

Schuyler Hamilton

History Of The National Flag Of The United States Of America
by Schuyler Hamilton

ISBN: 978-93-62209-34-4

Published by

DOUBLE 9 BOOKS

2/13-B, Ansari Road
Daryaganj, New Delhi – 110002
info@double9books.com
www.double9books.com
Tel. 011-40042856

This book is under public domain

ABOUT THE AUTHOR

Schuyler Hamilton, an esteemed historian and scholar, presents his magnum opus "History of the National Flag of the United States of America." This comprehensive work offers a meticulous examination of the evolution, symbolism, and significance of the American flag throughout the nation's history. Drawing from extensive research and a deep appreciation for patriotic symbolism, Hamilton delves into the origins of the flag, tracing its development from the Revolutionary War era to the present day. In his masterpiece, Hamilton skillfully navigates through pivotal moments in American history, such as the design of the first flag by Betsy Ross, the addition of stars and stripes to represent new states, and the various iterations of the flag's design over time. With meticulous attention to detail and rich historical context, Hamilton sheds light on the enduring symbolism of the flag as a beacon of freedom, unity, and national identity. Through engaging narrative and vivid imagery, "History of the National Flag of the United States of America" not only educates readers about the flag's history but also inspires a deep sense of pride and reverence for this iconic symbol of American values and ideals.

CONTENTS

PREFACE

As nearly as we can learn, the only origin which has been suggested for the devices combined in the national colors of our country is, that they were adopted from the coat of arms of General Washington. This imputed origin is not such as would be consonant with the known modesty of Washington, or the spirit of the times in which the flag was adopted. We have, therefore, been at some pains to collect authentic statements in reference to our national colors, and with these, have introduced letters exhibiting the temper of those times, step by step, with the changes made in the flag, so combining them as to form a chain of proof, which, we think, must be conclusive.

Should, however, the perusal of the following account of the origin and meaning of the devices in the national flag of our country, serve no other purpose than that of impressing more strongly upon the mind of the reader the importance and the prominence those who achieved our liberties and founded our government attached to the idea of Union, its preparation will not have been a futile labor.

Emblems and devices, adopted under high excitement of the public mind, are chosen as epitomes of the sentiments prevailing at the time of their adoption. Those of the days of our Revolution afford proofs far more striking than the most elaborate arguments, that, in the estimation of our forefathers, Union, and existence as a nation, were inseparable.

The prosecution of our subject has made it necessary for us to dwell upon those devices, and to develop those proofs.

INTRODUCTION

As a not uninteresting introduction to our research, we will glance at the history of standards, from their inception to the present time. We shall find that man's faculty of imitation has here, as elsewhere, found employment, modified in its operation by some cause peculiar to the nation whose standard chances to be under consideration.

Fosbroke, in his *Dictionary of Antiquities*, has furnished us with most of the information on this subject which is pertinent to our design. We shall add such comments as will tend to illustrate our conclusions. Under the head of standards, he writes:—

"The invention began among the Egyptians, who bore an animal at the end of a spear; but among the Græco-Egyptians, the standards either resemble, at top, a round-headed knife, or an expanded semicircular fan. Among the earlier Greeks, it was a piece of armor at the end of a spear; though Agamemnon, in Homer, uses a purple veil to rally his men, &c. Afterwards, the Athenians bore the olive and owl; the other nations the effigies of their tutelary gods, or their particular symbols, at the end of a spear. The Corinthians carried a *pegasus*, the Messenians their initial M, and the Lacedæmonians, Λ; the Persians, a golden eagle at the end of a spear, fixed upon a carriage; the ancient Gauls, an animal, chiefly a bull, lion, and bear. Sir S. R. Meyrick gives the following account of the Roman standards. 'Each *century*, or at least each *maniple* of troops, had its proper standard, and standard-bearer. This was originally merely a bundle of hay on the top of a pole; afterwards, a spear with a crosspiece of wood on the top; sometimes the figure of a hand above, probably in allusion to the word *manipulus*; and below, a small round or oval shield, generally of silver or of gold. On this metal plate were anciently represented the warlike deities Mars or Minerva; but after the extinction of the commonwealth, the effigies of the emperors or their favorites. It was on this account that the standards were called *numina legionum*, and held in religious veneration. The standards of different divisions had certain letters inscribed on them, to distinguish the one from the other. The standard of a legion, according to Dio, was a silver eagle, with expanded wings, on the top of a spear, sometimes holding a thunderbolt in its claws; hence the word *aquila* was used to signify a legion. The place for this standard was near the general, almost in the centre. Before the time of Marius, figures of other animals were used, and it was then carried in front of the first maniple of the *triarii*. The *vexillum*, or flag of the cavalry (that of the infantry being called *signum*; an eagle on a thunderbolt, within a wreath, in Meyrick, pl. 6, fig. 15), was, according to Livy, a square piece of cloth, fixed to a crossbar on the end of a spear. The *labarum*, borrowed by the Greek emperors from the Celtic tribes, by whom it was called *llab*, was similar to this, but with the monogram of Christ worked upon it. Thus Sir S. R. Meyrick. The dragon, which served for an ensign to barbarous nations, was adopted by the Romans, probably from the mixture of auxiliaries with the legions. At first, the dragon, as the general ensign of the barbarians, was used as a trophy by the Romans, after Trajan's conquest of the Dacians. The dragons were embroidered in cotton, or silk and purple. The head was of metal, and they were fastened on the tops of spears, gilt and tasselled, opening the mouth wide, which made their long tails, painted with different colors, float in the wind. They are seen on the Trajan column and the arch of Titus, and are engraved. The *draconarii*, or ensigns, who carried them, were distinguished by a gold collar. From the Romans, says Du Cange, it came to the Western Empire, and was long, in England, the chief standard of our kings, and of the dukes of Normandy. Matthew Paris notes its being borne in wars which portended destruction to the enemy. It was pitched near the royal tent, on the right of the other standards, where the guard was kept. Stowe adds, that the dragon-standard was never used but when it was an absolute intention to fight; and a golden dragon was fixed, that the weary and wounded might repair thither, as to a castle, or place of the greatest security. Thus far for the dragon-standard. To return, Vigetius mentions *pinnæ*, perhaps *aigrettes* of feathers, of different colors, intended for signals, rallying-points, &c. Animals, fixed upon plinths, with holes through them, are often found. They were ensigns intended to be placed upon the ends of spears.

"Count Caylus has published several; among others two leopards, male and female. Ensigns upon colonial coins, if accompanied with the name of the legion, *but not otherwise*, show that the colony was founded by the veterans of that legion. There were also standards called *pila*, or *tufa*, consisting of bucklers heaped one above the other.

"The ancient Franks bore the tiger, wolf, &c., but soon adopted the eagle from the Romans. In the second race, they used the cross, images of saints, &c. The *fleur-de-lis* was the distinctive attribute of the king.

"Ossian mentions the standard of the kings and chiefs of clans, and says that it (the king's) was blue studded with gold. This is not improbable, for the Anglo-Saxon ensign was very grand. It had on it *the white horse*, as the Danish was distinguished by the *raven*. They were, however, differently formed from the modern, being parallelograms, fringed, and borne, sometimes at least, upon a stand with four wheels. A standard upon a car was, we have already seen, usual with the ancient Persians. Sir S. R. Meyrick admits that it was of Asiatic origin, first adopted by the Italians, and introduced here in the reign of Stephen. That of Stephen is fixed by the middle upon a staff, topped by a cross *pattée* (wider at the ends than in the middle), has a cross *pattée* itself on one wing, and three small branches shooting out from each flag. It appears from Drayton, that the main standard of Henry V. at the battle of Agincourt was borne upon a car; and the reason which he assigns is, that it was too heavy to be carried otherwise. Sir S. R. Meyrick adds, that it preceded the royal presence. Edward I. had the arms of England, St. George, St. Edmond, and St. Edward, on his standards. The flag or banner in the hands of princes, upon seals, denotes sovereign power, and was assumed by many lords in the twelfth and thirteenth centuries."

We observe that the invention of standards is ascribed to the Egyptians. Layard, in "Nineveh, and its Remains," says of the standards of the Assyrians:—

"Standards were carried by the charioteers. In the sculptures, they have only two devices: one, a figure (probably that of the divinity) standing on a bull, and drawing a bow; the other, two bulls running in opposite directions," probably, as is stated in a note, the symbols of war and peace.

"These figures are inclosed in a circle, and fixed to the end of a long staff ornamented with streamers and tassels." Here we see the early use of pendants as emblems of supreme authority. In our own day, we frequently hear, Commodore — —'s broad pendant was hoisted on the ship — —. In Queen Anne's time, on the union of England and Scotland, we find the use of pendants by the ships of her subjects, expressly prohibited in the following words: "*Nor any kind of pendants whatsoever,* or any other ensign than the ensign described in the side or margent hereof, which shall be worn instead of the ensign before this time [1707] usually worn in merchant vessels." In reference to the flags of the national vessels, the following language is used: "Our flags, jacks, and pendants, which, *according to ancient usage,* have been appointed to a distinction for our ships." Every one will observe the distinction made in the case of the pendants, which were absolutely prohibited to the subjects. We return now to the consideration of the standards of the Assyrians. "The standards seem to have been partly supported by a rest in front of the chariot, and a long rod or rope connected them with the extremity of the pole. In a bas-relief of Khorsabad, this rod is attached to the top of the standard."[1]

The reader will have observed what Fosbroke says of the introduction into England of a standard borne on a car, that it was in imitation of the eastern nations. In the case of the Romans, the force of this habit was even more strikingly illustrated. They at first used a bundle of bay or straw; as they extended their conquests over the neighboring colonists from Greece, and doubtless from Egypt, they assumed the wolf and other animals. The wolf, perhaps, referred to the foster-mother of Romulus. As they extended their conquests further, they borrowed the custom of the Greeks, of placing a shield with the image of a warlike deity upon it on a spear, still, however, retaining the reference to the *manipulus* in the hand, above it.

In the time of Marius, they adopted the eagle with the thunderbolt in its claws, the emblem of Jove. We are also told that different divisions had certain letters, frequently the name of the commander, inscribed on their standards. This practice was also introduced among the Romans from Greece. It was introduced among the Grecians by Alexander the Great, who observed it among the Persians and other eastern nations. Intoxicated with his triumphs, when he began to claim for himself a divine origin, he caused a standard to be prepared, inscribed with the title of "Son of Ammon," and planted it near the image of Hercules, which, as that of his tutelary deity, was the ensign of the Grecian host. In the same way, the Franks borrowed the eagle from the Romans.

The same holds good of the dragon-standard, which, borrowed from the Dacians and other barbarians, was for a long time the standard of the Western Empire, of England, and of Normandy.

After the Crusades, however, the cross seems to have taken a prominent place on the standards and banners of European nations.

The double-headed eagle of Russia and Austria originated among the Romans, to indicate the sovereignty of the world. When the empire of the Cæsars was divided into the Western and Eastern Empires, this standard continued to be used in both those divisions. From the Eastern Empire it passed into the standard of Russia, on the marriage of Ivan I. with a Grecian princess. From the Western, with the title of Roman Emperor, it passed to Austria.

From the above, we cannot fail to perceive, in the past as well as in the present, the tendency, throughout the world, to imitation, in the adoption of national ensigns; also, that the adoption of a particular ensign marked some epoch in the history of the particular nation which adopted it.

Thus the various changes in the Roman standard marked the epochs of their conquest, first of the Greeks, then of the Barbarians. The adoption of the eagle by the Franks, their conquest of the Romans. The cross, the era of the Crusades. The double-headed eagle of Russia, the marriage of the Czar to the heiress of the Eastern Empire. That of Austria, the investiture of the emperors of Germany with the title of Roman Emperor. The present union of the crosses of St. George, St. Andrew, and St. Patrick, in the British ensign, reverting to the Crusades, in the members composing it, more directly refers to the union, first, of England and Scotland into the united kingdom of Great Britain, and more recently, to the union of the kingdoms of Great Britain and Ireland, and hence is called *The Great Union*.

The eagle of France, marked her republican era.

Having thus observed, in the adoption of ensigns by the principal nations of the world, the prevalence of certain general rules, viz.: A reference to their deity; the habit of imitating the ensigns of nations from which they sprung, or which they conquered; the custom of marking, by their standards, some epoch in their history; or these customs in combination, may we not expect to find, in the adoption of our National Ensign, that it is not wholly an exception to these general rules?

THE NATIONAL FLAG OF THE UNITED STATES OF AMERICA

Adopting these general principles, we find ourselves, in attempting to give a satisfactory account of the origin, adoption, and meaning of the devices embodied in the National Flag of the United States, obliged to describe the principal flags displayed during the Revolution, which resulted in the independence of those States; to give some account of the flags used by the colonists prior to that Revolution; and to notice, though in a cursory manner, the national flag of the mother country.

To facilitate the consideration of our subject, we shall arrange the flags, mention of which we have met with, as displayed during our Revolution, in a table, chronologically; and shall number them, according to the date of the notice of them, 1, 2, 3, 4, &c., beginning in 1774.

In this Table, we shall give their distinguishing devices; noticing them, when necessary, more at length as we proceed.

TABLE OF THE ABOVE FLAGS

1. "Union Flags."[2]—These flags are very frequently mentioned in the newspapers, in 1774, but no account is given of the devices upon them. To establish these devices, will be one of the principal objects of this inquiry.

2. The standard of the Connecticut troops.—A letter, dated Wethersfield, Connecticut, April 23, 1775, says: "We fix upon our standards and drums the colony arms, with the motto, '*Qui transtulit sustinet,*' round it, in letters of gold, which we construe thus: 'God, who transplanted us hither, will support us.'"[3] The standards of the different regiments were distinguished by their color. Act of Provincial Congress of Connecticut, July 1, 1775: "One standard for each regiment *to be distinguished by their color, as follows, viz.: for the seventh, blue; for the eighth, orange.*"[4]

3. The flag unfurled by General Israel Putnam, on Prospect Hill, July 18, 1775, which is thus described in a letter, dated

"Cambridge, July 21, 1775.

"Last Saturday, July 15, the several regiments quartered in this town being assembled upon the parade, the Rev. Dr. Langdon, President of the College, read to them 'A Declaration, by the Representatives of the United Colonies of North America now met in General Congress at Philadelphia, setting forth the causes and necessity of taking up arms.' It was received with great applause; and the approbation of the army, with that of a great number of other people, was immediately announced by three huzzas. His Excellency, the General, with several other general officers, &c., were present on the occasion."

"Last Tuesday morning, July 18, according to orders issued the day before by Major-General Putnam, all the continental troops under his immediate command assembled at Prospect Hill, when the Declaration of the Continental Congress was read; after which, an animated and pathetic address to the army was made by the Rev. Mr. Leonard, chaplain to General Putnam's regiment, and succeeded by a pertinent prayer, when General Putnam gave the signal, and the whole army shouted their loud *amen* by three cheers; immediately upon which a cannon was fired from the fort, and the standard lately sent to General Putnam was exhibited, flourishing in the air, bearing this motto; on one side, 'An Appeal to Heaven,' and, on the other side, '*Qui transtulit sustinet.*'

"The whole was conducted with the utmost decency, good order, and regularity, and the universal acceptance of all present; and the *Philistines*, on Bunker's Hill, heard the shout of the *Israelites*,[5] and, being very fearful, paraded themselves in battle array."[6]

This flag bore on it the motto of Connecticut, "*Qui transtulit sustinet*," and the motto, "An Appeal to Heaven;" the latter of which is evidently adopted from the closing paragraph of the "Address of the Provincial Congress of Massachusetts, to their brethren in Great Britain," written shortly after the battle of Lexington, which ended thus: 'Appealing to Heaven for the justice of our cause, we determine to die or be free;' and which motto, under the form 'Appeal to Heaven,' combined with a pine-tree, constituted the motto and device on the colors of the Massachusetts colonial cruisers. In this combination of the mottoes of Connecticut and Massachusetts, one can scarcely fail to perceive the germ of the emblem of union which was introduced into the flag, which, January 2, 1776, replaced the flag we have described above, on Prospect Hill.

From the following notice of the flag displayed by General Putnam, July 18, 1775, we learn that it was a red flag. Before, however, giving the notice, we will state that, as early as the time of the Romans, a red flag was the signal of defiance or battle; thus, we are told: "When a general, after having consulted the auspices, had determined to lead forth his troops against the enemy, a red flag was displayed on a spear from the top of the *Prætorium*,[7] which was the signal to prepare for battle."[8] This accords with the account given of the display of the above flag, and corroborates the fact mentioned in the following extract from a letter of a captain of an English transport to his owners in London:—

"Boston, Jan. 17, 1776.

"I can see the rebels' camp very plain, whose colors, a little while ago, were entirely red; but, on the receipt of the king's speech (which they burnt), they have hoisted the Union Flag, which is here supposed to intimate the union of the provinces."[9]

He probably could not perceive the mottoes referred to in the preceding letter, owing to the distance.

4. The flag used at the taking of Fort Johnston, on James's Island, September 13, 1775.—"Colonel Moultrie, September 13 [1775], received an order from the Council of Safety for taking Fort Johnston, on James's Island." [S.C.] "A flag being thought necessary for the purpose of signals, Colonel Moultrie, who was requested by the Council of Safety to procure one, had a large blue flag made, with a crescent in one corner, to be in uniform with the troops. This was the first American flag displayed in South Carolina."[10]

Of the crescent, we have the following interesting account:—

"As is well known, the crescent, or, as it is usually designated, the *crescent montant*, has become the symbol of the Turkish Empire, which has thence been frequently styled the Empire of the Crescent. This symbol, however, did not originate with the Turks. Long before their conquest of Constantinople, the crescent had been used *as emblematic of sovereignty*, as may be seen from the still-existing medals struck in honor of Augustus, Trajan, and others; and it formed from all antiquity the symbol of Byzantium. On the overthrow of this empire by Mohammed II., the Turks, regarding the crescent, which everywhere met their eye, as a good omen, adopted it as their chief bearing."[11] It was, doubtless, "as the emblem of sovereignty," that it was adopted by Colonel Moultrie.

5. The flag of the floating batteries.—Colonel Joseph Reed to Colonel Glover and Stephen Moylan, says: "Head-quarters, October 20, 1775: Please

to fix upon some particular color for a flag, and a signal by which our vessels may know one another. What do you think of a flag with a white ground, a tree in the middle, the motto, 'Appeal to Heaven?' This is the flag of our floating batteries."[12]

6. The flag called *The Great Union Flag*, hoisted January 2, 1776, the day which gave being to the new army.—General Washington's letter of January 4, 1776, to Joseph Reed.[13] This flag, which we shall designate in this way, was the basis of our National Flag of the present day.

7. The flag presented by Colonel Gadsden, a member of the Naval Committee of the Continental Congress, to the Provincial Congress of South Carolina, February 9, 1776, as the standard to be used by the Commander-in-chief of the American Navy, "being a yellow field, with a lively representation of a rattlesnake in the middle, in the attitude of going to strike; and the words underneath, Don't tread on me."[14]

8. The flag of the cruisers of the colony of Massachusetts.—"And the colors to be a white flag with a green pine-tree, and an inscription, 'Appeal to Heaven.'"—Resolution of Massachusetts Provincial Congress, April 29, 1776.[15]

9. The National Flag of the United States, "The Stars and Stripes," adopted as such by a Resolution of Congress, passed June 14, 1777.—"*Resolved*, That the flag of the Thirteen United States be thirteen stripes, alternate red and white; that the Union be thirteen stars, white, in a blue field, representing a new constellation."[16]

This Resolution, though passed June 14, 1777, was not made public until September 3, 1777.[17]

With this Table before us, we shall proceed to consider certain badges intimately connected with the devices on the national flag of England, afterwards embodied in the national flag of Great Britain, a modification of which we shall show was, for a time, the flag of the United States, and the basis of the "Stars and Stripes."

"In the first crusade, the Scots, according to Sir George Mackenzie, were distinguished by the Cross of St. Andrew; the French, by a white cross; and the Italians, by a blue one. The Spaniards, according to Columbiere, bore a red cross, which, in the third crusade (A.D. 1189), was appropriated by the French, the Flemings using a green cross, and the English a white one. The adherents of Simon Montfort, the rebellious earl of Leicester, assumed the latter as their distinguishing mark, thus making the national cognizance the badge of a faction.

Pl. I.

"The cross of St. George has been the badge, both of our kings and the nation, at least from the time of Edward III. Its use was for a while nearly superseded by the roses, but revived upon the termination of the wars between the rival houses. It still continues to adorn the banner of England."[18]

Of the arms and banner of St. George, we have the following account: "Saynte George, whyche had whyte arms with a red cross." (Fig. 1, Plate I.)

"This blessed and holy martyr Saynte George is patrone of the realme of England; and ye crye of men of warre."[19]

"With reference to the cross of St. George, Sir N. H. Nicholas observes: 'That in the fourteenth and subsequent centuries, even if the custom did not prevail at a much earlier period, every English soldier was distinguished by wearing that simple and elegant badge over his armor.'

"The following extract," he adds, "from the ordinances made for the government of the army with which Richard II. invaded Scotland in 1386, and which were also adopted by Henry V., will best show the regulations on the subject.

"Also, that everi man of what estate, condition, or nation thei be of, so that he be of oure partie, bere a signe of the armes of Saint George, large, both before and behynde, upon parell that yf he be slayne or wounded to deth, he that hath so done to him shall not be put to deth, for default of the cross that he lacketh. And that non enemy do bere the same token or cross of St. George, notwithstanding if he be prisoner, upon payne of deth."

"The banner of St. George is white, charged with the red cross."[20]

"Banner. A banner is a square flag painted or embroidered with arms, and of a size proportioned to the rank of the bearer."[21]—See the Banner of St. George, Fig. 2, Plate I.

We now come to the description of the arms and banner of Saint Andrew. The cross of St. Andrew is called a saltire, and is thus described:—

"Saltire, or *saltier*. This honorable ordinary probably represents the cross whereon St. Andrew was crucified."[22]

"Andrew, S., the Apostle: the patron saint of Scotland.

"The arms attributed to him, and emblazoned on the banner bearing his name, are azure, a saltire argent."[23]—See Fig. 3, Plate I., Arms of Saint Andrew; and for the banner of Saint Andrew, Fig. 4, Plate I.

"Union Jack: the national flag of Great Britain and Ireland.

"The ancient national flag of England was the banner of St. George (argent, a cross gules), to which the banner of St. Andrew (azure, a saltire argent), was united (instead of being quartered, according to ancient custom), in pursuance of a royal proclamation, dated April 12, 1606. An extract from this proclamation follows:—

"Whereas, some difference hath arisen between our subjects of South and North Britain, travelling by seas, about the bearing of their flags: for the avoiding of all such contentions hereafter, we have, with the advice of our council, ordered, that henceforth all our subjects of this Isle and kingdom of Great Britain, and the members thereof, shall bear in their maintop the red cross, commonly called St. George's Cross, and the white cross, commonly called St. Andrew's Cross, joined together, according to a form made by our heralds, and sent by us to our admiral, to be published to our said subjects; and in their foretop our subjects of South Britain shall wear the red cross only, as they were wont; and the subjects of North Britain, in their foretop, the white cross only, as they were accustomed."[24]

The union of the crosses described above may naturally be called the *king's colors*, though in fact, as James was king both of Scotland and England, the national flags of either of those kingdoms would also be the king's colors, in an extended sense; but would be likely to be designated as the red or white crosses, or the crosses of St. George or St. Andrew, while this form prepared by the heralds, and only prescribed for "subjects travelling by seas," would be by those subjects called, *par excellence*, the king's colors.

"There is," says Sir N. H. Nicholas, "every reason to believe that the flag arranged by the heralds on this occasion was the same as, on the union with Scotland [1707], became the national banner." It may be emblazoned azure, a saltire argent surmounted by a cross gules, edged of the second. (See Fig. 5, Plate I.) The white edging was no doubt intended to prevent one color from being placed upon another; but this precaution was, to say the least, unnecessary; for surely no heraldic rule would have been broken, if the red cross had been placed upon the white satire. The contact of the red cross and blue field would have been authorized by numerous precedents. This combination was constituted the national flag of Great Britain by a royal proclamation, issued July 28, 1707.[25]

"No further change was made until the union with Ireland, January 1, 1801, previous to which instructions were given to combine the banner of St. Patrick (argent, a saltire gules) with the crosses of St. George and St. Andrew. In obedience to these instructions, the present National Flag of Great Britain and Ireland was produced."[26]—See Fig. 6, Plate I.

We would observe that, as this last form of the *union* was only adopted in 1801, which was the first time that a change was made in the flags proscribed in 1707, it is only of interest as completing the account of the Union Jack.

"The word Jack is most probably derived from the surcoat, charged with a red cross, anciently used by the English soldiery. This appears to have been called a jacque, whence the word jacket, anciently written jacquit."[27]

We desire to impress this last remark upon the mind of the reader, as, in the course of our inquiry, we shall meet more than once with allusions to the "Jack," the "St. George's Jack," &c., and to invite special attention to the fact that the badge on the clothes of the soldiery furnished a badge to the flag of their country. Thus the cross of St. Andrew, worn by the Scots, was emblazoned on the banner of Scotland, and the cross of St. George, worn by the English soldiery, was emblazoned on the banner of England.

This last, the national flag of England, the Red Cross flag, has now, for us, especial interest.

A singular circumstance furnishes us with proof that this Red Cross flag was in use in the colonies. We find in the "Journal of John Winthrop, Esq., the first governor of the Colony of Massachusetts Bay," the following memoranda in reference to it:—

"Anno 1634, November 5.] At the Court of Assistants, complaint was made by one of the country (viz., Richard Brown, of Watertown, in the name of the rest), that the ensign at Salem was defaced, viz.: one part of the red cross taken out. Upon this, an attachment was issued against Richard Davenport, ensign-bearer, to appear at the next court to answer. Much matter was made of this, as fearing it would be taken as an act of rebellion, or of like high nature, in defacing the king's colors;" [*i.e.* the Banner of St. George;] "though the truth were, it was done upon this opinion, that the red cross was given to the King of England, by the pope, as an ensign of victory, and so a superstitious thing, and a relic of antichrist. What proceeding was hereupon, will appear after, at next court in the first month; for by reason of the great snows and frosts, we used not to keep courts in the three winter months."[28]

"Anno 1685, mo. 1, 4.] A General Court at Newtown."

"Mr. Endecott was called to answer for defacing the cross in the ensign; but, because the court could not agree about the thing, whether the ensigns should be laid by, in regard that many refused to follow them, the whole case was deferred till the next general court; and the commissioners for military affairs gave order, in the mean time, that all ensigns should be laid aside," &c.[29]

"Anno 1685, mo. 3, 6.] A General Court was held at Newtown, where John Haynes, Esq., was chosen governor; Richard Bellingham, Esq., deputy governor; and Mr. Hough, and Mr. Dummer, chosen assistants to the former; and Mr. Ludlow, the late deputy, left out of the magistracy. The reason was, partly, because the people would exercise their absolute power, &c., and partly by some speeches of the deputy, who protested against the election of the governor as void, for that the deputies of the several towns had agreed upon the election before they came, &c. But this was generally discussed, and the election adjudged good."[30]

"Mr. Endecott was also left out, and called into question about the defacing the cross in the ensign; and a committee was chosen, viz.: every town chose one (which yet were voted for by all the people), and the magistrates chose four, who, taking the charge to consider the offence, and the censure due to it, and to certify the court, after one or two hours time, made report to the court, that they found the offence to be great, viz.: rash and without discretion, taking upon him more authority than he had, and not seeking advice of the court, &c.; uncharitable, in that he, judging the cross, &c., to be a sin, did content himself to have reformed it at Salem, not taking care that others might be brought out of it also; laying a blemish, also, upon the rest of the magistrates, as if they would suffer idolatry, &c., and giving occasion to the state of England to think ill of us. For which they adjudged him worthy admonition, and to be disabled for one year from bearing any public office; declining any heavier sentence because they were persuaded he did it out of tenderness of conscience, and not of evil intent."[31]

"The matter of altering the cross in the ensign was referred to the next meeting (the court having adjourned for three weeks), it being propounded to turn it to the red and white rose, &c."

[We have seen, under our first notice of the Cross of St. George, that "its use was, for a while, nearly superseded (in England) by the roses, but revived upon the termination of the wars between the rival houses."] "And every man was to deal with his neighbors to still their minds, who stood so stiff for the cross, until we should fully agree about it, which was expected, because the ministers had promised to take pains about it, and to write into England to have the judgment of the most wise and godly there."[32]

"Anno 1635, mo. 12, 1.] At the last General Court it was referred to the military commissioners to appoint colors for every company; who did accordingly, and left out the cross in all of them, appointing the king's arms to be put into that of Castle Island, and Boston to be the first company."[33]

"Anno 1636, mo. 8, 15.] Here arrived a ship called the St. Patrick, belonging to Sir Thomas Wentworth [afterwards the great Earl of Strafford], deputy of Ireland [*i.e.* viceroy], one Palmer, master. When she came near Castle Island, the lieutenant of the fort went aboard her and made her strike her flag, which the master took as a great injury, and complained of it to the magistrates, who, calling the lieutenant before them, heard the cause and declared to the master that he had no commission so to do. And because he had made them strike to the fort (which had then no color abroad), they tendered the master such satisfaction as he desired, which was only this, that the lieutenant, aboard their ship, should acknowledge his error, that so all the ship's company might receive satisfaction, lest the lord deputy should have been informed that we had offered that discourtesy to his ship which we had never offered to any before."

"Mo. 8, 31.] One Miller, master's mate in the Hector, spake to some of our people aboard his ship, that, because we had not the king's colors at our fort, we were all traitors and rebels, &c. The governor sent for the master, Mr. Ferne, and acquainted him with it, who promised to deliver him to us.

Whereupon, we sent the marshal and four sergeants to the ship for him, but the master not being aboard they would not deliver him; whereupon, the master went himself and brought him to the court; and, the words being proved against him by two witnesses, he was committed. The next day the master, to pacify his men, who were in a great tumult, requested he might be delivered to him, and did undertake to bring him before us again the day after, which was granted him, and he brought him to us at the time appointed. Then, in the presence of all the rest of the masters, he acknowledged his offence, and set his hand to a submission, and was discharged."

We will break the thread of this extract to introduce this curious paper, which, taken from the *Colonial Record,* i. 179, we, find given at length in a note to Winthrop's *New England.*

"Whereas I, Thomas Millerd, have given out most false and reproachful speeches against his majesty's loyal and faithful subjects, dwelling in the Massachusetts Bay in America, saying that they were all traitors and rebels, and that I would affirm so much before the governor himself, which expressions I do confess (and so desire may be conceived) did proceed from the rashness and distemper of my own brain, without any just ground or cause so to think or speak, for which my unworthy and sinful carriage being called in question, I do justly stand committed. My humble request, therefore, is that, upon this my full and ingenuous recantation of this my gross failing, it would please the governor and the rest of the assistants to accept of this my humble submission, to pass by my fault, and to dismiss me from further trouble; and this, my free and voluntary confession, I subscribe with my hand, this 9th June, 1686."

We now resume our extract from Winthrop.

"Then the governor desired the masters that they would deal freely, and tell us, if they did take any offence, and what they required of us. They answered, that in regard they should be examined upon their return, what colors they saw here; they did desire that the king's colors might be spread at our fort. It was answered, we had not the king's colors. Thereupon, two of them did offer them freely to us." This was about June, 1636, and we have seen that it was only in the year 1635, that the commissioners for military affairs had ordered the red cross ensigns to be laid aside; hence, it is altogether improbable that they could not have procured one of these, but, what we have styled the king's colors *par excellence*, being prescribed only for ships, was not likely to be owned by the colonial authorities. Its device, a modification of the cross, about which the question had arisen, might possibly have served as a device to relieve the tenderness of the consciences of the authorities, and would also enable the masters to say, on their return, that they had seen the king's colors spread at the castle at Boston.

As we see above, "it was answered we had not the king's colors. Thereupon, two of them did offer them freely to us. We replied, that for our part, we were fully persuaded that the cross in the ensign was idolatrous, and, therefore, might not set it up in our ensign; but, because the fort was the king's, and maintained in his name, we thought his own colors might be spread there. So the governor accepted the colors of Captain Palmer, and promised they should be set up at Castle Island. We had conferred over night with Mr. Cotton, &c., about the point. The governor, and Mr. Dudley, and Mr. Cotton, were of opinion that they might be set up at the fort upon this distinction, that it was maintained in the king's name. Others, not being so persuaded, answered that the governor and Mr. Dudley, being two of the council, and being persuaded of the lawfulness, &c., might use their power to set them up. Some others being not so persuaded, could not join in the act, yet would not oppose, as being doubtful, &c."[34]

"Anno 1636, mo. 4, 16.] The governor, with consent of Mr. Dudley, gave warrant to Lieutenant Morris, to spread the king's colors at Castle Island, when the ships passed by. It was done at the request of the masters of the ten ships which were then here; yet with this protestation, that we held the cross in the ensign idolatrous, and, therefore, might not set it up in our own ensigns; but this being kept as the king's fort, the governor and some others were of opinion that his own colors might be spread upon it. The colors were given us by Captain Palmer, and the governor, in requital, sent him three beaver-skins."[35]

The following order of the Court of Massachusetts, leads us to conclude that these colors, or those containing the king's arms, were continued in use until they were likely to bring the colony under the displeasure of the Parliament of England, which, in arms against the king, used the Red Cross flag, or St. George's banner. We then find the colony of Massachusetts giving orders on this matter as follows:—

"MASSACHUSETTS RECORDS, 1651[36]

"Forasmuch as the court conceives the old English colors now used by the Parliament of England to be a necessary badge of distinction betwixt the English and other nations in all places of the world, till the state of England shall alter the same, which we much desire, we being of the same nation, have, therefore, ordered that the captain of the castle shall presently advance the aforesaid colors of England upon the castle upon all necessary occasions."

These extracts show the importance attached to *colors* in those times.

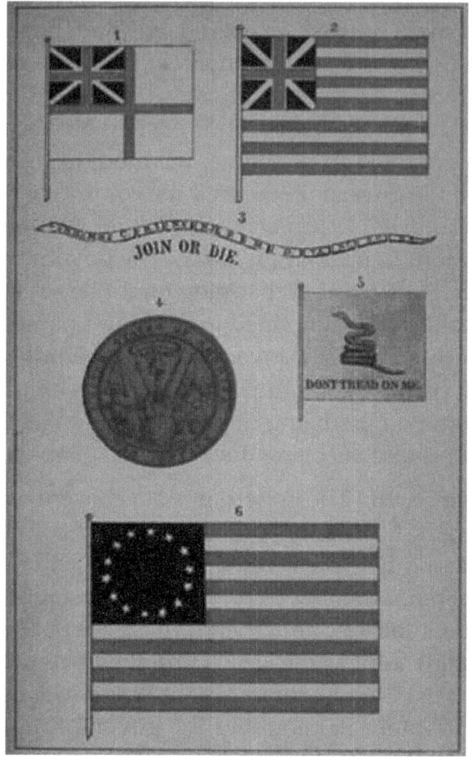

Pl. II.

This question, and indeed all questions, as to the flags to be used both at sea and land by the subjects of Great Britain, and the dominions thereunto belonging, were, however, set at rest, by the 1st article of the treaty of union between Scotland and England, from which fact the flags then prescribed were called *Union flags*.

"Act of Parliament ratifying and approving the treaty of the two kingdoms of Scotland and England, Jan. 16, 1707."

"I. Article. That the two kingdoms of Scotland and England shall, upon the first day of May next, ensuing the date hereof, and forever after, be united into one kingdom by the name of Great Britain; and that the ensigns armorial of the said united kingdom be such as her majesty shall appoint; and the crosses of St. Andrew and St. George be conjoined in such manner as her majesty shall think fit, and used in *all* flags, banners, standards, and ensigns, both at sea and land."[37]

Under the head of Union Jack, we have shown how these crosses were conjoined. We now give a portion of the proclamation of July 28, 1707, referred to in that account of the Union Jack.

"BY THE QUEEN: PROCLAMATION

"Declaring what ensigns and colors shall be borne at sea in merchant ships, and vessels belonging to any of her majesty's subjects of Great Britain, and the dominions thereunto belonging.

"Anne R.

"Whereas, by the first article of the treaty of union, as the same hath been ratified and approved by several acts of Parliament, the one made in our Parliament of England, and the other in our Parliament of Scotland, it was provided and agreed that the ensigns armorial of our kingdom of Great Britain be such as we should appoint, and the crosses of St. George and St. Andrew conjoined in such manner as we should think fit, and used in all flags, banners, standards, and ensigns, both at sea and land, we have therefore thought fit, by, and with the advice of our privy council, to order and appoint the ensign described on the side or margent hereof [see Fig. 7, Plate I.], to be worn on board of all ships or vessels belonging to any of our subjects whatsoever; and to issue this, our royal proclamation, to notify the same to all our loving subjects, hereby strictly charging and commanding the masters of all merchant ships and vessels belonging to any of our subjects, whether employed in our service or otherwise, and all other persons whom it may concern, to wear the said ensign on board their ships and vessels. And whereas, divers of our subjects have presumed, on board their ships, to wear our flags, jacks, and pendants, which, according to ancient usage, have been appointed to a distinction for our ships, and many times thinking to avoid the punishment due for the same, have worn flags, jacks, and pendants in shape and mixture of colors, so little different from ours, as not without difficulty to be distinguished therefrom, which practice has been found attended with manifold inconveniences: for prevention of the same for the future, we do, therefore, with the advice of our privy council, hereby strictly charge and command all our subjects whatsoever, that they do not presume to wear on any of their ships or vessels, our jack, commonly called the Union Jack, nor any pendants, nor any such colors as are usually borne by our ships without particular warrant for their so doing from us, or our high admiral of Great Britain, or the commissioners for executing the office of high admiral for the time being; and do hereby further command all our loving subjects, that, without such warrant as aforesaid, they presume not to wear on board their ships or vessels, any flags, jacks, pendants, or colors, made in imitation of ours, or any kind of pendant, whatsoever, or any other ensign, than the ensign described in the side or margent hereof, which shall be worn instead of the ensign before this time usually worn in merchant vessels. Saving that, for the better distinction of such ships as shall have commissions of letters of mart or reprisals against the enemy, and any other ships or vessels which may be employed by principal officers and commissioners of our navy, the principal officers of our ordnance, the commissioners for victualling our navy, the commissioners for our customs, and the commissioners for transportation for our service—relating particularly to those offices our royal will and pleasure is, That all such ships as have commissions of letters of mart and reprisals, shall, besides the colors or ensign hereby appointed to be worn by merchant ships, wear a red jack, with a Union Jack described in a canton at the upper corner thereof, next the staff [see Fig. 1, Plate II.], and that such ships and vessels as shall be employed for our service by the principal officers and commissioners of our navy, &c. [same enumeration as before], shall wear a red jack with a Union Jack in a canton at the upper corner thereof, next the staff, as aforesaid; and in the other part of the said jack, shall be described the seal used in such of the respective offices aforesaid, by which the said ships and vessels shall be employed. [This flag was the same as Fig. 1, Plate II., except the seal of the office by which employed.] And we do strictly charge and command, &c., (and the residue orders, seizure of vessels not obeying this proclamation, by wearing other ensigns, &c., and to return the names of such ships and vessels, and orders strict inquiry into any violation of the proclamation, and then directs it to take effect in the Channel or British seas and in the North

Sea, after twelve days from the date of the proclamation, and from the mouth of the Channel unto Cape St. Vincent after six weeks from the date, and beyond the cape, and on this side the equinoctial line, as well in the ocean and Mediterranean as elsewhere, after ten weeks from the date, and beyond the line, after the space of eight months from the date of these presents.)

"Given at our court at Windsor, the 28th day of July, in the sixth year of our reign.[38]

"GOD SAVE THE QUEEN"

In a description of Boston Harbor, in 1720, thirteen years after the date of this proclamation, we learn that, "to prevent any possible surprise from an enemy, there is a light-house built on a rock appearing above water, about three long leagues from the town, which, in time of war, makes a signal to the castle, and the castle to the town, by hoisting and lowering the Union flag so many times as there are ships approaching."[39]

After having given the first article of the treaty, and the above proclamation, this description is only useful as proving that the term "Union Flag" was the familiar one applied to describe the flags established under the union, as well in the colonies as the mother country, and explains the following note in Frothingham's *Siege of Boston*.

Frothingham says: "In 1774, there are frequent notices of Union flags in the newspapers, but I have not met with any description of the devices on them."[40] After the history of Union flags already given, this will not appear surprising; for who, in our day, speaking of the "Stars and Stripes," would pause to describe its devices. We, however, are inclined to the opinion that the flags spoken of in the newspapers, referred to by Mr. Frothingham, were the ensigns described in the proclamation of Queen Anne, as being the common ensign of the commercial marine of "Great Britain, and the dominions thereof." For, as such, they must have been more easily procurable than the Union Jacks, and more familiar to the people, and therefore would appeal with most force to the popular sentiment.

That this was the case in the colony of New York, we learn from the following: "In March, 1775, 'a Union flag with a red field' was hoisted at New York upon the liberty-pole, bearing the inscription 'George Rex, and the Liberties of America,' and, upon the reverse, 'No Popery.'"[41] With the exception of the mottoes, this was the same flag as is represented, Fig. 7, Plate I.

Frothingham gives us to understand that they were displayed on liberty-poles and on the famous "Liberty Tree" on Boston Common. In this connection, we will quote a few lines from a letter, dated Philadelphia, December 27, 1775, to show the temper of the public mind at that time, and to indicate the name given to the colonies, whose flag we are now about to consider.

"TO THE PEOPLE OF NORTH AMERICA:

"Philadelphia, December 27, 1775.

"Those who have the general welfare of the United English Colonies in North America sincerely at heart, who wish to see peace restored, and her liberties established on a solid foundation, may, at present, be divided into two classes, viz.: those who 'look forward to an independency as the only state in which they can perceive any security for our liberties and privileges,' and those who 'think it not impossible that Britain and America may yet be united.'

"If the present struggle should end in the total independence of America, which is not impossible, every one will acknowledge the necessity of framing what may be called the 'Constitution of the United English Colonies.' If, on the other hand, it should terminate in a reunion with Great Britain, there yet appears so evident a necessity of such a constitution that every good man must desire it."[42]

This letter shows the importance the Union of the Colonies, lately entered into, held in the mind of the public. Prior to its being entered into, its necessity was thus forcibly indicated to the public mind. The newspapers commonly bore the device of a disjointed snake, represented as divided into thirteen portions. Each portion bearing the initials of one of the colonies, and under it the motto, "Join, or die." Thus impressed, we can readily perceive how naturally they seized upon the flag in use in the mother country and its dominions, as an emblem of union among the members of that mother country, to indicate the necessity of it among the colonies, and, by displaying it from liberty-poles, &c., indicated the object for which union was necessary, viz.: to secure the liberty of British subjects.

The first authentic account of the display of the Union flag, as the flag of the united colonies, is from the pen of General Washington, in a letter addressed to Colonel Joseph Reed, his military secretary.

"Cambridge, January 4, 1776.

"Dear sir: We are at length favored with a sight of his majesty's most gracious speech, breathing sentiments of tenderness and compassion for his deluded American subjects. The echo is not yet come to hand, but we know what it must be; and, as Lord North said (and we ought to have believed and acted accordingly), we now know the ultimatum of British justice. The speech I send you. A volume of them was sent out by the Boston gentry; and, farcical enough, we gave great joy to them, without knowing or intending it; for, on that day, the day which gave being to the new army, but before the proclamation came to hand, we had hoisted the Union flag in compliment to the united colonies. But, behold! it was received in Boston as a token of the deep impression the speech had made upon us, and as a signal of submission. So we hear, by a person out of Boston, last night. By this time, I presume, they begin to think it strange that we have not made a formal surrender of our lives."

[From *Philadelphia Gazette*], note to the above, in *American Archives*.

"Philadelphia, January 15, 1776.

"Our advices conclude with the following anecdote: That, upon the king's speech arriving at Boston, a great number of them were reprinted and sent out to our lines on the 2d of January, which, being also the day of forming the new army, The Great Union Flag was hoisted on Prospect Hill, in compliment to the United Colonies. This happening soon after the speeches were delivered at Roxbury, but before they were received at Cambridge, the Boston gentry supposed it to be a token of the deep impression the speech had made, and a signal of submission. That they were much disappointed at finding several days elapse without some formal measure leading to a surrender, with which they had begun to flatter themselves."

We observe, in General Washington's letter, that the Americans, "farcical enough," "without knowing or intending it," led the Boston gentry to imagine them about to surrender, because a Union flag was displayed, which was only displayed in compliment to the United Colonies on the day the army, organized under the orders of Congress, *subsequent* to the union of the thirteen colonies, came into being. And, in the extract from the newspaper account of this, that the flag was displayed on Prospect Hill, and that it must have been a peculiarly marked Union flag, to be called

The Great Union Flag. As this was the name given to the national banner of Great Britain, this indicates this flag as the national banner of the United Colonies. Lieutenant Carter, a British officer, very naturally explains both these circumstances. He was on Charlestown Heights, and says: January 26, 1776: "The king's speech was sent by a flag to them on the 1st inst. In a short time after they received it, they hoisted an Union flag (above the continental with thirteen stripes) at Mount Pisgah; their citadel fired thirteen guns, and gave the like number of cheers."[43]

This account of the flag, from Lieut. Carter, is corroborated by the following from the captain of an English transport, to his owners in London, when taken in connection with the extract subjoined to it, taken from the *British Annual Register* for 1776. The captain writes:—

"Boston, Jan. 17, 1776.

"I can see the rebels' camp very plain, whose colors, a little while ago, were entirely red; but, on the receipt of the king's speech (which they burnt), they have hoisted the Union Flag, which is here supposed to intimate the union of the provinces."[44]

The *Annual Register* says: "The arrival of a copy of the king's speech, with an account of the fate of the petition from the Continental Congress, is said to have excited the greatest degree of rage and indignation among them; as a proof of which, the former was publicly burnt in the camp; and they are said, on this occasion, to have changed their colors from a plain red ground, which they had hitherto used, to a flag with thirteen stripes, as a symbol of the number and union of the colonies."[45]

We have already shown that the first flag spoken of in both the above accounts (Flag No. 3) in our Table, bore certain mottoes; and not being precise in the description of the flag, which for months had been displayed before their eyes, we may expect inaccuracies in the description of a flag newly presented to them, and which, even to an officer on Charlestown Heights, who, as appears, was at some pains to describe it, appeared to be *two* flags; and remembering that this flag was supposed to be displayed on the receipt of the king's speech, the following account of the colors of British regiments explains why it was especially regarded by the British as a token of submission.

"The kings, or *first* color of every regiment, is to be the Great Union throughout.

"The *second* color is to be the color of the facing of the regiment, with the Union in the upper canton, except those regiments which are faced with red, white, or black.

"The first standard, Guidon, or color of regiments of the line, is not to be carried by any guard but that of the King, Queen, Prince of Wales, Commander-in-chief, or Admiral of the Fleet, being of the royal family; and, except in those cases, it is always to remain with the regiment."[46]

From the above we see that, to the mind of a British officer, the Union flag, supposed to have been displayed in connection with the receipt of the king's speech, above a flag with thirteen stripes, would indicate an acknowledgment of the supremacy of the king over the United Colonies, supposed to be represented in the thirteen stripes.

Without further proof, therefore, we may conclude that the "Union" flag, displayed by General Washington, was the union of the crosses of St. George and St. Andrew, with thirteen stripes through the field of the flag. (See Fig. 2, Plate II.)

On the evacuation of Boston by the British, this standard was, on the entrance of the American army into Boston, carried by Ensign Richards.[47]

While we may fairly infer from General Washington's letter, that this emblem of union had presented itself to his mind as such, we may also infer from his not describing its accompanying devices, to mark the compliment to the United Colonies, that he supposed Colonel Joseph Reed, his military secretary, fully acquainted with them; and from this we may conclude Colonel Reed had something to do with its preparation. This conclusion is strengthened by the fact, that Colonel Joseph Reed was Secretary to the Committee of Conference sent by Congress to arrange with General Washington the details of the organization of the army, which went into being January 2, 1776. And, at the very time that Committee was in session at the camp at Cambridge, we find Colonel Reed having the subject of flags under consideration. To the reply to a letter written by him at that time, we may possibly trace the origin of the use of a modification of the British ensign, a drawing of which is given under Queen Anne's proclamation before quoted, as the flag of the United Colonies. And we shall give good reasons to conclude that this modification consisted in applying to its red field a sufficient number of white stripes, to divide the whole into thirteen stripes, alternate red and white, as above shown; and we will show the propriety of this by establishing the fact that a *stripe* was the badge of rank in the ununiformed army that assembled about Boston in defence of liberty.

Colonel Joseph Reed, Secretary to the Committee of Conference from Congress, and Military Secretary of General Washington, the Committee being then in session, wrote, October 20, 1776: "Please fix upon some particular color for a flag and a signal by which our vessels may know one another.[48] What do you think of a flag with a white ground, a tree in the middle, the motto, 'Appeal to Heaven?' This is the flag of our floating batteries." To which Colonels Glover and Moylan replied, October 21, 1775: "That as Broughton and Selman, who sailed that morning, had none but their old colors, they had appointed the signal by which they could be known by their friends to be 'the ensign up to the maintopping lift."[49]

This ensign, which is called their "old colors," must have been the ensign spoken of and described in Queen Anne's proclamation. (See Fig. 7, Plate I.) Since we have seen *one* ensign prescribed 1707, for the merchant ships and vessels of Great Britain, and the dominions thereunto belonging, and that no change was made until 1801. This being the case, the ensign of the colonial cruisers, inasmuch as they were armed merchant vessels, must have been the British ensign displayed at the maintopping lift. There were several reasons for this; the most forcible of which were, that it being usual to have no special place for the display of the national ensign at sea, but the custom being to exhibit it in such part of the vessel from which it could be most conveniently observed by the strange sail (on which occasion only it was worn at sea), to adopt a particular place for its display would be to give it a new character; one peculiarly happy for the then state of affairs, as it would betray the *English* transports to the colonial cruisers, and would not betray the *Colonial* cruisers to the British ships of war, as "the maintopping lift" must have been such a position as would not attract the attention of those not in the secret. This reply of the gentlemen charged with the continental or colonial cruisers, would readily have suggested a modification of the British ensign for the ensign of the United Colonies of North America; for the transition, in the adoption of a flag, from a particular place for the display of a particular flag, to some modification of the same flag, was both natural and easy; especially, as a slight modification of this flag would enable them to indicate the number of colonies, while the emblem of union would happily indicate the union of those colonies, and at the same time would have justified them in saying, in their address of December 6, 1775, "Allegiance to our king. Our words have ever avowed it, our conduct has ever been in keeping with it," as having acknowledged their dependence on the mother country, even in the flag with which they were to struggle against her.

Before we proceed to consider the origin of the stripes, we shall give an account of the same flag as displayed on the fleet fitted out at Philadelphia about this time, so as to fix, beyond a doubt, this emblem of *union*. As a preliminary, we will give a short extract of the sailing orders given to Benedict Arnold's fleet,[50] when he set out on his expedition to Canada. They may be found at length in Major Meigs's journal of that expedition.

"1st Signal." "For speaking with the whole fleet, *ensign* at maintopmast head."

"2d Signal." "For chasing a sail, ensign at foretopmast head."

"6th Signal." "For boarding any vessel, Jack at maintopmast head, and the whole fleet to draw up in a line as near as possible."

The Jack, or Union, or Union Jack, as it was and is called, was and is, to this day, in the navy of Great Britain, the flag of the admiral of the fleet; and was probably, as such, worn by the vessel of the commander-in-chief of this expedition, and its use probably suggested the adoption of a standard for the commander-in-chief of the first American fleet, Flag No. 7, in our table. The date of sailing of the above fleet was Sept. 19, 1775, before the letter of Colonels Glover and Moylan, speaking of the "old colors," was written (the date of the latter was Oct. 21, 1775), and the use of the terms jack and ensign strengthens the conclusion that the term "old colors" meant British colors, for we shall find, in the orders of the first American fleet, that the ensign and jack are called the striped ensign and Jack.

In this connection, we give a few extracts from the sailing orders of the first American fleet, "given the several captains in the fleet, at sailing from the Capes of Delaware, Feb. 17, 1776."[51]

"Sir: You are hereby ordered to keep company with me, if possible, and truly observe the signals given by the ship I am in."

"In case you are in any very great danger of being taken, you are to destroy these orders and your signals."

SIGNALS FOR THE AMERICAN FLEET BY DAY

"For chasing: For the whole fleet to chase, a red pennant at the foretopmast head." We have already said that, since the time of the Romans, a red flag has been the signal to prepare for battle.

"For seeing a strange vessel: Hoist the ensign, and lower and hoist it as many times as you see vessels, allowing two minutes between each time."

Supposing this *ensign* to be a Union flag, observe the similarity between this signal and that for the lighthouse and castle in Boston Harbor in 1720; "the lighthouse," as we have already stated, "in time of war makes a signal to the castle, and the castle to the town, by hoisting and lowering the Union flag so many times as there are ships approaching."

"For the Providence to chase: A St. George's ensign with stripes at the mizzen peak."

"For a general attack, or the whole fleet to engage, the standard at the maintopmast head, with the *striped* Jack and ensign at their proper places."

Now let us look at some of the descriptions of the colors of this fleet, both by American and British writers.

SAILING OF THE FIRST AMERICAN FLEET

"Newbern, North Carolina, February 9, 1776.

"By a gentleman from Philadelphia, we have received the pleasing account of the actual sailing from that place of the first American fleet that ever swelled their sails on the Western Ocean, &c.

"This fleet consists of five sail, fitted out from Philadelphia, which are to be joined at the capes of Virginia by two more ships from Maryland, and is commanded by Admiral Hopkins, a most experienced and venerable sea captain."

"They sailed from Philadelphia amidst the acclamations of thousands assembled on the joyful occasion, under the display of a Union flag, with thirteen stripes in the field, emblematical of the thirteen United Colonies."[52]

And the following extract from a letter, dated New Providence, West Indies, of which Island Admiral Hopkins took prisoner the governor, &c.[53]

This letter was kindly furnished by Colonel Peter Force, editor of the *American Archives*, and may be found in the *London Ladies' Magazine*, vol. vii. July 1776, p. 390.

"New Providence, May 18, 1776.

"The colors of the American fleet were striped under the *Union*, with thirteen strokes, called the United Colonies, and their standard, a rattlesnake; motto—'Don't tread on me.'"

The following extract was furnished by the same gentleman, to whom I cannot too warmly return my thanks for the facilities and assistance he has afforded me.

"Williamsburg, Va., April 10, 1776.

"The Roebuck [a British cruiser] has taken two prizes in Delaware Bay, which she decoyed within her reach, by hoisting a *Continental Union Flag*."

Reference to this letter not obtained, but in support of its correctness, see affidavit of Mr. Barry, master's mate, ship Grace, captured by the Roebuck, to be found in the *Pennsylvania Evening Post*, June 20, 1776, vol. ii. No. 221.

It is unnecessary to multiply proof on this subject. The term *union*, in these accounts, both by American and British writers, at sea and land, by the interpretation we give it, explains and harmonizes all of them. We therefore proceed to consider the other and what may be called the distinctive devices—we mean the stripes on this Continental Union Flag.

Under the head of Ensign (*Brande's Dictionary*), we are told: "Men of war carry a red, white, or blue ensign, according to the color of the flag of the admiral." By the 1st Article of the union between England and Scotland, we have seen that the ensigns, both "at sea and land," were to embody the union of the crosses of St. George and St. Andrew conjoined; hence the colors, red, white, &c., only apply to the field of the ensign.

In the extract from the King's Regulations for the British Army, we have shown that the ensign of the different regiments differed in color according as the facings of the uniforms of the particular regiments to which they belonged differed. We have seen, in the Crusades, the different nations were distinguished by different colored crosses on their surcoats, from which the particular colored cross was transferred to the national banners of at least Scotland and England. Here the striking distinction was color. The same practice prevailed at the time of the Revolution in the colonies.—See the Proceedings of the Provincial Congress of Connecticut, "July 1, 1775. One standard for each regiment, distinguished by their color, as follows, viz.: For the seventh, blue; for the eighth, orange."[54]

With this practice of nations, then, before them, and evidently applied by them, viz.: that of applying some badge of distinction in use in their armies to their national banner, combined with that of indicating different portions of their armies by different colors for their flags; and of two nations, when uniting, adopting as a common ensign something to indicate their union, and still preserve the original banners (both as to devices and color), under which they had respectively achieved signal triumphs, especially as this last example was that of the mother country, we may expect to see the colonies carrying out this practice in their Union flag.

They were British colonies: and, as we have shown, they used the British Union, but now, they were to distinguish their flag by its color from other British ensigns, preserve a trace of the colors under which they had previously fought with success, and, at the same time, represent this combination in some form peculiar to themselves.

The mode of distinction by color could not well be applied by the United Colonies in a single color, as the simpler and most striking were exhausted in application to British ensigns; but, if applied, must have been used in a complex form or combination of colors. This being the case, stripes of color would naturally be suggested as being striking, as enabling them to show the number and union of the colonies, *as preserving the colors of the flags previously used by them*; and also the badge of distinction, which, at the time of the adoption of this flag, marked the different grades in the ununiformed army before Boston. Hence, probably, the name, *The Great Union Flag*, given to it by the writer in the *Philadelphia Gazette*, before quoted, doubtless Colonel Joseph Reed, inasmuch as this flag indicated, as respected the Colonies, precisely what the Great Union Flag of Great Britain indicated respecting the mother country.

The only point that now remains for us to establish is, that a stripe or ribbon was the badge in common use in the army of the colonists before Boston. In proof of this, we quote the following extracts from the orders of General Washington.

"Head-Quarters, Cambridge, July 14, 1775.

("Countersign, Inverness. Parole, Halifax.)

"There being something awkward as well as improper in the general officers being stopped at the outposts, asked for passes by the sentries, and obliged, often, to send for the officer of the guard (who, it frequently happens, is as much unacquainted with the persons of the generals as the private men), before they can pass in or out, it is recommended to both officers and men, to make themselves acquainted with the persons of all officers in general command, and, in the mean time, to prevent mistakes, the general officers and their aides-de-camp will be distinguished in the following manner: The commander-in-chief, by a light blue ribbon worn across his breast, between his coat and waistcoat; the majors and brigadiers general by a pink ribbon worn in like manner; the aides-de-camp, by a green ribbon."[55]

"Head-Quarters, Cambridge, July 28, 1775.

("Parole, Brunswick. Countersign, Princeton.)

"As the continental army have unfortunately no uniforms, and consequently many inconveniences must arise from not being able always to distinguish the commissioned officers from the non-commissioned, and the non-commissioned from the privates, it is desired that some badges of distinction may be immediately provided; for instance, the field officers may have red or pink colored cockades in their hats, the captains yellow or buff, and the subalterns green. They are to furnish themselves accordingly. The sergeants may be distinguished by an epaulette or stripe of red cloth sewed upon the right shoulder, the corporals by one of green."[56]

"Head-Quarters, Cambridge, July 24, 1775.

("Parole, Salisbury. Countersign, Cumberland.)

"It being thought proper to distinguish the majors from brigadiers general, by some particular mark for the future, the majors general will wear a broad purple ribbon."

Having thus established the use of the stripe as a badge of distinction, we have completed our proofs in reference to the Union flag displayed by General Washington before Boston, January 2, 1776. And to perceive how simple and natural is the deduction of the ensign of the army and fleet of the United English Colonies of North America, from the national ensign of Great Britain, it is only necessary to compare Fig. 7, Plate I. and Fig. 2, Plate II.

Having made some observations in reference to the mottoes on several of the flags given in our table, we would now invite attention to the religious character of those on the colonial flags, viz.: *Qui transtulit sustinet*, and an "Appeal to Heaven." In the famous effort of colonial vigor, which, resulting in the capture of Louisburg, surprised the world in 1745, we learn, from Belknap's *History of New Hampshire*, vol ii. p. 157, that the flag used bore the motto, *Nil desperandum Christo Duce*. A motto furnished by the celebrated George Whitfield. This last flag, under the treaty of union, must have been an Union flag, probably, similar to the British ensign above given, or perhaps with a white field, to which color the New England people were partial (see the colors of the Massachusetts cruisers, Flag No. 8, in our table), with the motto above given inscribed on the field.

May we not conclude that, when the flags embodying such mottoes were dispensed with, some reference to them would still be preserved, as would be the case by preserving in the flag which replaced them the colors of the flags laid aside?

THE RATTLESNAKE UNION FLAG

The letter previously quoted, dated New Providence, May 13, 1776, says: "And their standard, a rattlesnake;" motto—"Don't tread on me." This *standard* is thus described, viz.:—

"In Congress, February 9, 1776.

"Colonel Gadsden presented to the Congress an elegant standard, such as is to be used by the Commander-in-chief of the American Navy, being a yellow field, with a lively representation of a rattlesnake in the middle, in the attitude of going to strike, and the words underneath, 'Don't tread on me.'[57]

"*Ordered*, That the said standard be carefully preserved and suspended in the Congress room."

Before I proceed, I shall offer one or two remarks on this device of the rattlesnake, to show that it also, as well as the British crosses, was an emblem of union, and that it was seized upon as one *then* (December, 1775) in use, and familiar.

In 1754, in the *Philadelphia Gazette*, when Benjamin Franklin was editor of that paper, an article appeared, urging *union* among the colonies as a means of insuring safety from attacks of the French. This article closed with a wood-cut of a snake divided into parts, with the initials of one colony on each division, and the motto, "Join, or die," underneath, in capital letters. [58] (See Fig. 3, Plate II.)

When union among the colonies was urged, in 1774-6, as a mode of securing their liberties, this device, a disjointed snake, divided into *thirteen* parts, with the initials of a colony on each division, and the motto, "Join, or die," was adopted as the head-piece of many of the newspapers. When the union of the colonies took place, this was changed, for the head-pieces of the newspapers, into the device adopted on the standard, viz.: a rattlesnake in the attitude of going to strike, and into an *united* snake. (Under both forms of this device, was the motto, "Don't tread on me.")

The seal of the War Department is the only public instrument in use, exhibiting evidence of the rattlesnake's having played an important part as a device in the American Revolution. The old seal of 1778, and the more modern seal now in use, both bear the rattlesnake (with its rattles as the emblem of union), and a *liberty cap* in contiguity with it; the *liberty cap* enveloped by the body, so that the opened mouth may defend the *rattles,* and liberty cap, or *union* and liberty, with the motto, "This we'll defend." (See Fig. 4, Plate II.)

The following account of this device, supposed to be from the pen of Benjamin Franklin, indicates fully why it was adopted, and will be found in the *American Archives*, vol. iv. p. 468.

"Philadelphia, December 27, 1775.

"I observe on one of the drums belonging to the marines now raising, there was painted a rattlesnake, with this motto under it, 'Don't tread on me.' As I know it is the custom to have some device on the arms of every country, I suppose this may have been intended for the arms of America; and, as I have nothing to do with public affairs, and as my time is perfectly my own, in order to divert an idle hour, I sat down to guess what could have been intended by this uncommon device. I took care, however, to consult, on this occasion, a person who is acquainted with heraldry, from whom I learned that it is a rule, among the learned in that science, 'that the worthy properties of the animal, in the crest-born, shall be considered;' he likewise informed me that the ancients considered the serpent as an emblem of wisdom; and, in a certain attitude, of endless duration—both which circumstances, I suppose, may have been had in view. Having gained this intelligence, and recollecting that countries 'are sometimes represented by animals peculiar to them,' it occurred to me that the rattlesnake is found in no other quarter of the world beside America, and may, therefore, have been chosen on that account to represent her.

"But then, 'the worthy properties' of a snake, I judged, would be hard to point out. This rather raised than suppressed my curiosity, and having frequently seen the rattlesnake, I ran over in my mind every property by which she was distinguished, not only from other animals, but from those of the same genus or class of animals, endeavoring to fix some meaning to each, not wholly inconsistent with common sense.

"I recollected that her eye excelled in brightness that of any other animal, and that she has no eye-lids. She may, therefore, be esteemed an emblem of vigilance. She never begins an attack, nor, when once engaged, ever surrenders. She is, therefore, an emblem of magnanimity and true courage. As if anxious to prevent all pretensions of quarrelling with her, the weapons with which nature has furnished her she conceals in the roof of her mouth; so that, to those who are unacquainted with her, she appears to be a defenceless animal; and even when those weapons are shown and extended for defence, they appear weak and contemptible; but their wounds, however small, are decisive and fatal. Conscious of this, she never wounds till she has generously given notice, even to her enemy, and cautioned him against the danger of treading on her. Was I wrong sir, in thinking this a strong picture of the temper and conduct of America?

"The poison of her teeth is the necessary means of digesting her food, and at the same time is certain destruction to her enemies. This may be understood to intimate that those things which are destructive to our enemies, may be to us not only harmless, but absolutely necessary to our existence. I confess I was wholly at a loss what to make of the rattles, till I went back and counted them; and found them just thirteen, exactly the number of the colonies united in America; and I recollected, too, that this was the only part of the snake which increased in number.

"Perhaps it might be only fancy, but I conceited the painter had shown a half-formed additional rattle; which, I suppose, may have been intended to represent the province of Canada. 'Tis curious and amazing to observe how distinct and independent of each other the rattles of this animal are, and yet how firmly they are united together, so as never to be separated but by breaking them to pieces. One of these rattles singly is incapable of producing sound; but the ringing of thirteen together is sufficient to alarm the boldest man living. The rattlesnake is solitary, and associates with her kind only, when it is necessary for their preservation. In winter, the warmth of a number together will preserve their lives: while, singly, they would probably perish. The power of fascination attributed to her, by a generous construction, may be understood to mean, that those who consider the liberty and blessings which America affords, and once come over to her, never afterwards leave her, but spend their lives with her. She strongly resembles America in this, that she is beautiful in her youth, and her beauty increaseth with her age, 'her tongue also is blue, and forked as the lightning, and her abode is among impenetrable rocks.'

"Having pleased myself with reflections of this kind, I communicated my sentiments to a neighbor of mine, who has a surprising readiness at guessing at everything which relates to public affairs; and indeed, I should be jealous of his reputation in that way, was it not that the event constantly shows that he has guessed wrong. He instantly declared it as his sentiments, that the Congress meant to allude to Lord North's declaration in the House of Commons, that he never would relax his measures until he had brought America to his feet; and to intimate to his lordship, that if she was brought to his feet, it would be dangerous treading on her. But, I am positive he has guessed wrong, for I am sure that Congress would not condescend, at this time of day, to take the least notice of his lordship, in that or any other way. In which opinion, I am determined to remain, your humble servant."

The yellow flag, with the rattlesnake in the middle, and the words underneath, "Don't tread on me," (see Fig. 5, Plate II.,) the standard for the Commander-in-chief of the American Navy, was probably the flag referred to by Paul Jones, in his journal.

Paul Jones was commissioned first of the first lieutenants in the continental navy. "This commission, under the United Colonies, is dated the 7th of December, 1775, as first lieutenant of the Alfred. On board that ship, before Philadelphia, Mr. Jones hoisted the flag of America, with his own hands, the first time it was ever displayed, as the commander-in-chief embarked on board the Alfred." (Page 34, *Life and Correspondence of Paul Jones.*)

From the foregoing account, it will be perceived that the first flag adopted by the army of the colonists before Boston, was a red flag, with the mottoes, *Qui transtulit sustinet,* and "An Appeal to Heaven." By the combination of these mottoes, the union of Massachusetts and Connecticut, in defence of their outraged liberties, was doubtless intimated; and, taken in connection with those mottoes, the color of the flag indicated that, trusting in the God of battles, they defied the power of the mother country. About this time, too, the floating batteries, the germ of the navy subsequently organized, bore a white flag, with a green pine-tree, and the motto, "Appeal to Heaven." These flags were adopted before the union of the *thirteen* colonies was effected.

After that union, and upon the organization of the army and fleet, these flags were supplanted by one calculated to show to the world the union of the North American colonies among themselves, and as an integral part of the British Empire, and as such demanding the rights and liberties of British subjects. And a flag combining the crosses of St. George and St. Andrew united (the distinctive emblem of the United Kingdom of Great Britain), with a field composed of thirteen stripes, alternate red and white, the combination of the flags previously used in the camp, on the cruisers, and the floating batteries of the colonies, was adopted for this purpose, and called The Great Union Flag.

The union implied both the union of the colonies represented in the striped field, which was dependent upon it, and the nationality of those colonies. The thirteen stripes, alternate red and white, constituting the field of the flag, represented the body of that union, the number of the members which composed it, as well as the union of the flags, which had preceded this Great Union Flag.

We assume that the colors of those stripes were alternate red and white, inasmuch as those were the colors in the first flag of the United States, and we presume no change, not absolutely necessary, was made, in altering the flag of the United Colonies to that of the United States. There is no evidence of their being of that color, except the universally received tradition that such was the case.

The colors of those stripes, alternate red and white, indicated on the part of the colonies, thus represented as united, the defiance to oppression, symbolized by the red color of the flag of the army, and red field of the flag of the continental cruisers together, with the purity implied by the white flag of the floating batteries, of which the motto was, "Appeal to Heaven."

Lest these conclusions should seem far fetched, we would again advert to the fact, that in the present Union, or national flag of the United Kingdom of Great Britain and Ireland, not only are the crosses of St. George, St. Andrew, and St. Patrick united, but the colors of the fields of the banners of St. George, of England, St. Andrew, of Scotland, and St. Patrick, of Ireland, are preserved.

In the case of the colonies, everything that tended to call to mind previous triumphs would have been studiously preserved, and the red and white flags were identified with the successes of Bunker Hill, (for tradition says the flag on that occasion was red, and that a Whig told General Gage

that the motto was, "Come, if you dare,")[59] and the various successes of
the siege of Boston, prior to Jan. 2, 1776.

The use of the stripes, besides indicating the union of the above flags,
for the purpose before indicated, would, as a badge of distinction for the
Great Union Flag of the colonies, have carried the minds of those who were
marshalled under it back to the moment when the tocsin of war sounded
at Lexington—called them, "generals" as well as "private men,"—in the
garbs in which they were pursuing their peaceful avocations, to arms in
defence of liberty. And we of the present day should regard them as
hallowed, by having been employed by General Washington as the first
step towards introducing subordination into the army, which achieved our
independence. In those stripes we may perceive the necessity indicated of
the subordination of each State to the Union, while their equality under
the Union is also intimated, by there being nothing to indicate that any
particular State was represented by any particular stripe. There being seven
red stripes, doubtless arose from that being the color of the principal flags
represented in the combination of colors, for certainly the flags of the army
and cruisers must have had pre-eminence over that of the floating batteries.

The striped Union flag was the colonial colors, both at sea and land,
but there was also, as we have seen, a standard such as was used by the
commander-in-chief of the American navy, being a yellow field, with a
lively representation of a rattlesnake in the middle, in the attitude of going
to strike, and the words underneath, "Don't tread on me." The color of
the snake, as represented, was dark. This circumstance goes strongly to
prove the correctness of our conclusion, that the example of the mother
country was followed in the preparation of the flags of this period—for
the quarantine flag of the mother country was a *yellow* flag with a dark
spot, a representation of the plague-spot in the middle—those colors were,
doubtless, chosen for the rattlesnake flag, to indicate the deadly character of
the venom of the rattlesnake, and the danger of treading on it.

But we have before stated that the rattlesnake first appeared as a
snake divided into thirteen parts, each part marked with the initials of the
colony to which it corresponded, and beneath them the motto, "Join, or
die," indicating the necessity of union. And that, the union being effected,
the initials on the parts were dropped (thus indicating the equality of the
colonies under the Union), and the parts were united in the form indicated
in this standard, and beneath it the words, "Don't tread on me," implying
the consciousness of strength derived from that union, of which, we have
seen, the rattlesnake was an emblem indigenous to America, while at the
same time the serpent implies eternal duration. This, then, may properly be
called the Rattlesnake Union Standard, and the other, the Great Union, or

Striped Union Flag; and together they indicated that existence as a people was inseparable from union—the strength resulting from that union—the necessary subordination of each colony to the whole Union, the intimate connection of the colonies composing the Union, their equality and perpetuity under it, and the power of fascination in the Union and harmony in the colonies, which would draw everybody to America, and cause those who had once tasted the liberty and blessings she enjoys, never to leave her, but to "spend their lives with her."

Having thus described the flags of the United Colonies, and shown that they were emblematic of union, and hence called Union flags, in imitation of the prevailing custom of the mother country, we now proceed to consider the Flag of the United States, described in the following Resolution of Congress, passed June 14, 1777:—

> "*Resolved*, That the Flag of the Thirteen United States be thirteen stripes, alternate red and white: That the union be thirteen stars, white in a blue field, representing a new constellation."

This resolution was made public September 3, 1777; and Colonel Trumbull represents the flag made in pursuance of it as used at Burgoyne's surrender, October 17, 1777.

From the above resolution and what has preceded, it is apparent that the object of that resolution was simply to give the authorization of Congress to a color existing, so far as the stripes and part of the flag called the union were concerned; but it is worthy of remark that the character of the new emblem for that union is specially described as representing "a new constellation."

The use of some emblem of union different from the British crosses, the United States having declared themselves free and independent States, was eminently natural, but the description of the emblem substituted for them as "representing a new constellation," involves the idea that some constellation, in some way emblematic of union, had been presented to the minds of those adopting this resolution. It may be said that the adoption of a star, as the representative of a State, would naturally lead to the idea of a constellation; but, as the emblem to be altered was one of union, we are inclined to think that the first idea suggested was that of some constellation, which of itself implied union, and that the representation of a State by a star was involved in it.

The question that now arises is, was there any constellation which implied union? The answer is, there was the constellation Lyra. The next point is, to ascertain if the first flag displayed under this resolution bore that constellation. If not, in what form the stars were presented on that flag, and whether any connection can be traced between it and the constellation Lyra.

Let us first consider the fitness of the constellation Lyra to indicate union. In Charles Anthon's *Dictionary of Greek and Roman Antiquities*, we find the following account of the Lyra. He says: —

"Lyra. The Latin name *fides*, which was used for a lyre as well as a cithara, is probably the same as the Greek σφιδες, which, according to Hesychius, signifies gut-strings; but Festus takes it to be the same as *fides* (faith), *because the lyre was the symbol of harmony and unity among men.*" The quotation from the Astronomicon of Manilius, presented in the following letter from Mr. Charles Francis Adams, grandson of Mr. John Adams, confirms the attributes above ascribed to the lyre, and its corresponding constellation "Lyra."

Quincy, May 18, 1852.

Dear Sir: Your letter of the fourth came upon me unprepared to answer it without investigations, which I have ever since been hoping to pursue, but thus far in vain. Not a moment has been at my command since I received it, and as I am now expecting every moment to depart for Washington, I fear that I must give up all idea of doing more hereafter, at least in season for any object of yours.

With the exception of a few letters to and from Generals Green, Sullivan, Parsons, and Ward, there are no memorials remaining in my hands of my grandfather's services while chairman of the Board of War. He had no time to copy or record papers, so that very few are left. I am not aware of the existence of any journal or other record of the action of the body, nor of any further history of it than is given in his lately published diary. I am, therefore, wholly unable to give you any light upon the question of the origin of the American colors.

With regard to the other design, of the eagle, with the lyre on its breast, and the stars of the constellation Lyra, I can only say that I possess the seal which was the original form in which the device was presented. There it has the motto, *Nunc sidera ducit*, taken from the Astronomicon of Manilius, describing the effect of the Lyre of Orpheus,

"At Lyra diductis per cœlum cornibus inter Sidera conspicitur, qua quondam ceperat Orpheus Omne quod attigerat, cantu, manesque per ipsos Fecit iter, domuit que infernas carmine leges. Hinc cœlestis honos, similisque potentia causæ: Tunc silvas et saxa trahens, nunc sidera ducit, Et rapit immensum mundi revolubilis orbem."

II. 331-337.

It is my opinion that, although this last line does not appear, my father had it in his mind when applying the device to the American passport, but I have not had the leisure to look for any explanation he may have himself left of it. His papers are voluminous, and I have barely as yet glanced at any part of their contents. This must be my apology for sending you so unsatisfactory a reply.

I am, very respectfully, your obedient servant,

(Signed,) CHARLES FRANCIS ADAMS.

The following is a translation of the above quotation:—

Conspicuous among the stars, its horns wide spread over the heavens, is the Lyre, with which Orpheus was wont to captivate everything to which he addressed his song, and even made a journey through Hades itself, and put to sleep the infernal laws. Hence, its celestial honor; and, by the same power with which it then drew rocks and trees along, it now leads the stars, and *whirls along the immense orb of the revolving world.*

This last line shows that the constellation Lyra, as an emblem of union for the United States, would have been an amplification of the attribute of "fascination" ascribed to the Rattlesnake, as an emblem of union for the United States, in the account we have already given of the Rattlesnake as such, in describing the standard of the commander-in-chief of the American navy; for the constellation Lyra would not only imply "that those who consider the liberty and blessings which America affords, and once come over to her, never afterwards leave her, but spend their lives with her," but that by their union and harmony the United States would "whirl along the immense orb of the revolving world," to follow their example in their forms of government.

Having thus shown how appropriate the constellation Lyra would have been as an emblem of the union of the United States, we proceed to ascertain if the first flag displayed under the resolution of June 14, 1777, bore that constellation. In Trumbull's picture of the surrender of Burgoyne, and

Peale's picture of Washington, the thirteen stars are represented as arranged in a circle; it now remains to show the existence of some record exhibiting a connection between the constellation Lyra and the circle of thirteen stars.

We find this record on a form for a passport of the United States, prepared under Mr. John Quincy Adams, when Secretary of State, in 1820, which form is now in use. In adopting the form in question, the arms of the United States, previously used on U.S. passports, were replaced by a circle of thirteen stars surrounding an eagle, holding in his beak the constellation Lyra, and the motto, *Nunc sidera ducit*.

Mr. W. J. Stone, of Washington City, gives the following account of the preparation of the device above described, and presented in the vignette to the title-page. In it, the constellation Lyra is represented as radiating into a circle of thirteen stars.

Mount Pleasant, Washington City, May 8, 1852.

My Dear Sir: I find, on examination, that on the 25th of August, 1820, I engraved for the Department of State, by order of J. Q. Adams, Secretary of State, a plate for a passport, at the head of which was a spread eagle, drawn to encompass the constellation Lyra.

The drawing was made by me, according to particular verbal directions given by Mr. Adams. I have a distinct recollection of having submitted the drawing to Mr. Adams, for approval, previous to engraving.

Very respectfully, your obedt. servt.

(Signed,) W. J. STONE.

Had not this device been substituted, on the form for a United States passport, for the arms of the United States, by Mr. John Quincy Adams, we should not consider the constellation Lyra, radiating into a circle of thirteen stars, as having any special meaning; but as, at the time the circle of thirteen stars was introduced into the flag of the United States as an emblem of union, his father, Mr. John Adams, was chairman of the Board of War, we think it has.

On page 6, vol. iii. of the *Life and Writings of John Adams*, we find the following entry in his journal:—

"The duties of this Board kept me in continual employment, not to say drudgery, from the 12th of June 1776, till the 11th of November 1777." Again: "Other gentlemen attended as they pleased, but, as I was chairman, or as they were pleased to call it, president, I must never be absent."

A change being contemplated in the emblem of union in the flag, the Board of War would, doubtless, have had charge of the preparation of the substitute; and from the above, we perceive the chairman must have been particularly connected with its preparation.

We have thus presented the data upon which is based the conclusion that the constellation Lyra was originally proposed for the union of our Flag, in 1777, at the time the circle of thirteen stars was adopted. The reasons for that conclusion are the following:—

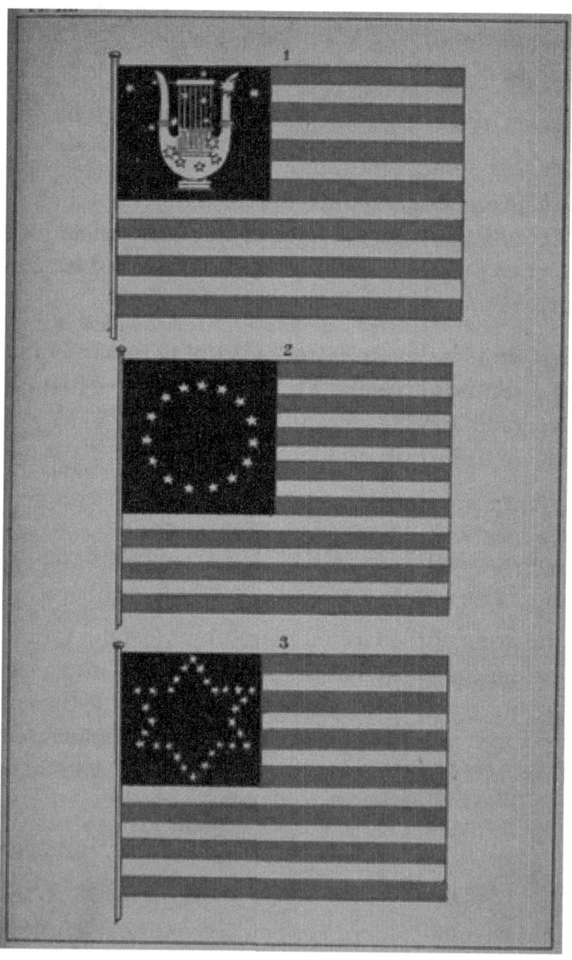

Pl. III.

It was a Union flag that was to be altered. The United States having become independent of Great Britain, the British emblem of union was no longer appropriate; some other emblem of union was to be substituted.

The constellation Lyra was a time-honored emblem of union. The language of the resolution of June 14, 1777, evidently has reference to such an emblem, representing a constellation. The Lyra was not adopted. A circle of thirteen stars was. At this time, Mr. John Adams was chairman of the Board of War.

Mr. John Adams's son became Secretary of State in 1820. Striking out the arms of the United States, he presented on the passport a device, representing the constellation Lyra radiating into a circle of stars—the stars thirteen in number. At this time there were twenty-one States in the Union—hence this circle of thirteen stars referred to an earlier day. The first instance of a circle of thirteen stars being used as a national device, was in the U. S. Flag, and its being presented on the passport must have referred to that use of it, as constituting it a well-known emblem of the United States, indicative of their union, while the constellation Lyra, occupying the centre of this circle, indicates the origin of the circle of stars, as an emblem of union "representing a new constellation," in that time-honored emblem of union. The other circumstances we have adduced point to Mr. John Adams as the source from which his son derived his information. We suppose the circle of stars was preferred to the Lyra because it indicated the perpetuity of the Union, which was distinctly intimated by the Rattlesnake Standard, laid aside when the flag of the United States, commonly called the Stars and Stripes, was adopted. It may not be improper to observe that these deductions are in keeping with the general rules, presented in our Introduction, as deduced from the practices of nations relative to national emblems.

Compare Fig. 6, Plate II., the Flag of the United States, as first presented under the resolution of June 14, 1777, with Fig. 1, Plate III., the flag as we suppose it to have been proposed when Mr. John Adams was chairman of the Board of War, and both of the above with the vignette to the title-page, the device introduced into the passport in *lieu* of the arms of the United States, by Mr. John Q. Adams, when Secretary of State.

In making these comparisons, the eagle, only adopted for the arms of the United States in 1782, must be kept out of view, or rather considered as having no part in the question about the stars.

In the preceding pages, we have established the origin of the part of the flag called "the union," also that of the circle of stars as an emblem for that union, together with that of the stripes, as clearly as analogy will enable us so to do. As corroborating the views we have advanced, we now present to the reader the reports on the adoption of the arms of the United States, copied by permission from unpublished records of the State Department, from which it appears that certain of those who prepared the devices for the Flag of the United States, were also engaged in the preparation of the device for a Great Seal.

"JOURNALS OF CONGRESS"

"1776—*page* 248.

"*July 4.* Dr. Franklin, Mr. J. Adams, and Mr. Jefferson, be a committee to prepare a device for a Great Seal for the United States of America.

"1776—*page* 321.

"*Aug. 10.* The Committee appointed to prepare the Device for a Great Seal for the United States brought in the same, with an explanation thereof; ordered to lie on the table.

"No. 1. *Copy of a Report made Aug. 10, 1776.*

"The Great Seal should on one side have the arms of the United States of America, which arms should be as follows:—

"The shield has six quarters, parts one, *coupé* two. The 1st or, a rose, enamelled gules and argent for England; the 2d argent, a thistle proper, for Scotland; the 3d verd, a harp or, for Ireland; the 4th azure a *flower-de-luce* or, for France; the 5th or, the imperial eagle, sable, for Germany; and the 6th or, the Belgic lion, gules for Holland, pointing out the countries from which the States have been peopled. The shield within a border gules entwined of thirteen scutcheons argent, linked together by a chain or, each charged with initial letters sable as follows: 1st, N.H.; 2d, M.B.; 3d, R.I.; 4th, C.; 5th, N.Y.; 6th, N.J.; 7th, P.; 8th, D.E.; 9th, M.; 10th, V.; 11th, N.C.; 12th, S.C.; 13th, G., for each of the thirteen independent States of America.

"Supporters dexter the Goddess Liberty, in a corselet of armor, alluding to the present times; holding in her right hand the spear and cap, and with her left supporting the shield of the States, sinister, the Goddess Justice, bearing a sword in her right hand, and in her left a balance.

"Crest. The eye of Providence in a radiant triangle, whose glory extends over the shield and beyond the figures. Motto: *E. Pluribus Unum.*

"Legend round the whole achievement. Seal of the United States of America, MDCCLXXVI.

"On the other side of the said Great Seal should be the following device:—

"Pharaoh sitting in an open chariot, a crown on his head and a sword in his hand, passing through the divided waters of the Red Sea in pursuit of the Israelites. Rays, from a pillar of fire in the cloud, expressive of the Divine presence and command, beaming on Moses, who stands on the shore, and, extending his hand over the sea, causes it to overthrow Pharaoh. Motto: *Rebellion to tyrants is obedience to God.*"

In regard to this Report, we observe Mr. John Adams was one of those engaged in preparing it. The emblems to represent countries were the rose for England, the thistle for Scotland, the harp for Ireland, &c. May not this train of ideas have suggested to his mind the lyre and its corresponding constellation to mark the Union of the United States of America in the flag of those States?

We observe the reference to the Sacred Volume in the device for the reverse of the proposed Seal. May not the idea of stars, as the representatives of dependent States, have been borrowed from the same source, and applied in the case of the flag as States dependent upon union, and thus constituting a constellation?

"March 25, 1779—page 101.

"Ordered, that the Report of the Committee on the Device of a Great Seal for the United States, in Congress assembled, be referred to a committee of three—Lovell, Scott, Houston."

This Committee made a Report, May 10. *Vide No. 2.*

"Original Report of May 10, 1779. No. 2."

"The seal to be four inches in diameter.

"On one side, the arms of the United States, as follows: The shield charged on the field, with thirteen diagonal stripes, alternate red and white. Supporters dexter, a warrior holding a sword; sinister, a figure representing Peace, bearing an olive-branch. The crest, a radiant constellation of thirteen stars. The motto: *Bello vel pace.* The legend round the achievement, *Seal of the United States.*

"On the reverse: The figure of Liberty, seated in a chair, holding the staff and cap. The motto: *Semper*. Underneath, MDCCLXXVI."

"*May 17, 1779—page* 149.

"The Report of the Committee on the Device of a Great Seal was taken into consideration, and, after debate,

"Ordered that it be recommitted."

"Report No. 2, on the Great Seal, as altered after recommitment.

"The Committee to whom was referred, on the 25th of March last, the report of a former committee on the Device of a Great Seal of the United States, in Congress assembled, beg leave to report the following description:—

"The Seal to be three inches in diameter.

"On one side, the arms of the United States, as follows: The shield charged in the field azure, with thirteen diagonal stripes, alternate rouge and argent, supporters; dexter, a warrior holding a sword; sinister, a figure representing Peace, bearing the olive-branch. The crest, a radiant constellation of thirteen stars. The motto. *Bello vel pace*. The legend round the achievement, *The Great Seal of the United States*.

"On the reverse: The figure of Liberty, seated in a chair, holding the staff and cap. The motto: *Virtute perennis*. Underneath, MDCCLXXVI.

"A drawing of the Seal is annexed. No. 3, May 10, 1780.

"A miniature of the face of the Great Seal to be prepared, of half the diameter, to be affixed as the less Seal of the United States."

We have not thought it worth while to present the drawing above referred to.

"*Device for an Armorial Atchievement for the United States of North America, blazoned agreeably to the laws of Heraldry, proposed by Mr. Barton, A.M.*

"Arms.—Paleways of [60]thirteen pieces, argent and gules; a chief azure: the escutcheon placed on the breast of an American (the bald-headed) eagle, displayed proper; holding in his beak a scroll, inscribed with the motto, viz.:—

and in his dexter talon a palm or an olive-branch; in the other a bundle of thirteen arrows; all proper.

"For the Crest.—Over the head of the eagle, which appears above the escutcheon, a glory, or, breaking through a cloud, proper, and surrounding thirteen stars forming a constellation, argent on an azure field.

"In the exergue of the Great Seal—

"Jul. IV. MDCCLXXVI."

"In the margin of the same—

"Sigil. Mag. Reipub. Confoed. Americ."

"Remarks.—The escutcheon is composed of the chief and pale, the two most honorable ordinaries; the latter represent the several States, all joined in one solid compact entire, supporting a chief, which unites the whole and represents Congress. The motto alludes to the Union. The colors or tinctures of the pales are those used in the Flag of the United States. White, signifies purity, innocence; red, hardiness and valor. The chief denotes Congress. Blue is the ground of the American uniform, and this color signifies vigilance, perseverance, and justice.

"The meaning of the crest is obvious, as is likewise that of the olive-branch and arrows.

"The escutcheon being placed on the breast of the eagle is a very ancient mode of bearing, and is truly imperial. The eagle *displayed*, is another heraldric figure; and, being borne in the manner here described, supplies the place of supporters and crest. The American States need no supporters but their own virtue, and the preservation of their Union through Congress. The pales in the arms are kept closely united by the chief, which last likewise depends on that Union, and strength resulting from it, for its own support—the inference is plain.

W. B."

"June 13, 1782."

Mr. Barton also presented the following:—

"A device for an armorial atchievement for the Great Seal of the United States of America, in Congress assembled, agreeably to the rules of heraldry, proposed by William Barton, A.M.

"Arms.—Barry of thirteen pieces, argent and gules, on a canton azure, and many stars disposed in a circle of the first; a pale or, surmounted of another, of the third; charged in chief, with an eye surrounded with a glory proper; and in the fess-point, an eagle displayed on the summit of a Doric column, which rests on the base of the escutcheon, both as the stars.

"Crest.—Or, an helmet of burnished gold damasked, grated with six bars, and surmounted of a cap of dignity, gules, turned up ermine, a cock armed with gaffs proper.

"Supporters.—On the dexter side; the genius of America (represented by a maiden with loose auburn tresses, having on her head a radiated crown of gold encircled with a sky-blue fillet, spangled with silver stars; and clothed in a long loose white garment, bordered with green. From her right shoulder to her left side a scarf, *semé* of stars, the tinctures thereof the same as in the canton; and round her waist a purple girdle, fringed or embroidered argent, with the word ' Virtue'—resting her interior hand on the escutcheon, and holding in the other the proper *Standard of the United States*, having a dove argent perched on the top of it.

"On the sinister side: a man in complete armor, his sword-belt azure, fringed with gold, his helmet encircled with a wreath of laurel, and crested with one white and two blue plumes; supporting with his dexter hand the escutcheon, and holding in the interior a lance, with the point sanguinated, and upon it a banner displayed, Vert., in the fess-point an harp stringed with silver, between a star in chief, two *fleurs-de-lis* in fess, and a pair of swords, in saltier, in basses, all argent. The tenants of the escutcheon stand on a scroll, on which is the following motto:—

'Deo Favente,'

which alludes to the *eye* in the arms, meant for the eye of Providence.

"Over the crest, in a scroll, this motto:—

which requires no comment.

"The thirteen pieces, barways, which fill up the field of the arms, may represent the several States; and the same number of stars, upon a blue canton, disposed in a circle, represent a new constellation, which alludes to the new empire formed in the world by the confederation of those States. Their disposition in the form of a circle, denotes the perpetuity of its continuance, the ring being the symbol of eternity. The eagle displayed, is the symbol of supreme power and authority, and signifies the Congress; the pillar upon which it rests is used as the hieroglyphic of fortitude and constancy, and its being of the Doric order (which is the best proportioned and most agreeable to nature), and composed of several members, or parts, all taken together, forming a beautiful composition of strength, congruity, and usefulness, it may, with great propriety, signify a well-planned government. The eagle being placed on the summit of the column is emblematical of the sovereignty of the government of the United States; and as further expressive of that idea, those two charges, or five and six azure, are borne in a pale which extends across the thirteen pieces into which the escutcheon is divided. The signification of the eye has been already explained. The helmet is such as appertains to sovereignty, and the cap is used as the token of freedom and excellency. It was formerly worn by dukes; says Guillien, *they had a more worthy government than other subjects.* The cock is distinguished for two most excellent qualities, viz., *vigilance* and *fortitude.*

"The genius of the American confederated Republic is denoted by the blue scarf and fillet glittering with stars, and by the tag of Congress which she displays. Her dress is white edged with green, colors emblematical of innocence and truth. Her purple girdle and radiated crown indicate her sovereignty; the word "Virtue," on the former, is to show that that should be her principal ornament; and the *radiated* crown, that no earthly crown shall rule her. The dove, on the top of the American standard, denotes the mildness and purity of her government.

"The knight in armor, with his bloody lance, represents the military genius of the American empire, armed in defence of its just rights. His blue belt and blue feathers, indicate his country, and the white plume is in compliment to our gallant ally. The wreath of laurel round his helmet is expressive of his success.

"The green field of the banner denotes youth and vigor; the harp[61] [with thirteen strings], emblematical of the several States acting in harmony and concert; the star *in chief* has reference to America, as *principal* in the contest; the two *fleurs-de-lis* are borne as a grateful[62] testimony of the *support* given to her by France, and the two swords, crossing each other, signify the state of war. This tenant and his flag relate totally to America at the time of her Revolution.

(Signed,) "WM. BARTON."

Mr. Middleton, Mr. Boudinot, and Mr. Rutledge, reported a modification of this, June 13, 1782, which was referred to the Secretary of the United States, in Congress assembled, to take order.

Device for a Great Seal, as adopted June 20, 1782.

"The Secretary of the United States in Congress assembled, to whom was referred the several reports of committees on the device of a Great Seal to take order, reports:—

"That the device for an armorial atchievement, and reverse of a Great Seal for the United States in Congress assembled, is as follows:—

"Arms.—Paleways, of thirteen pieces, argent and gules, a chief azure. The escutcheon on the breast of the American bald eagle, displayed proper, holding in his dexter talon an olive-branch, and in his sinister a bundle of thirteen arrows, all proper, and in his beak a scroll, inscribed with this motto: *E Pluribus Unum.*

"For The Crest.—Over the head of the eagle, which appears above the escutcheon, a glory, or, breaking through a cloud proper, and surrounding thirteen stars forming a constellation, argent on an azure field.

"Reverse.—A pyramid unfinished. In the zenith, an eye in a triangle, surrounded with a glory proper. Over the eye these words, *Annuit Cœptis.* On the base of the pyramid, the numerical letters, MDCCLXXVI., and underneath the following motto:

"Remarks and Explanations.—The escutcheon is composed of the chief and pale, the two most honorable ordinaries. The pieces paly, represent the several States all joined in one solid compact entire, supporting a chief, which unites the whole and represents Congress. The motto, alluding to this Union. The pales in the arms are kept closely united by the chief, and the chief depends on that union, and the strength resulting from it, for its support, to denote the confederacy of the United States of America, and the preservation of their Union through Congress.

"The colors of the pales are those used in the flag of the United States of America; white, signifies purity and innocence; red, hardiness and valor; and blue, the color of the chief, signifies vigilance, perseverance, and justice. The olive-branch and arrows denote the power of peace and war, which is exclusively vested in Congress. The constellation denotes a new State taking its place and rank among the sovereign powers. The escutcheon is borne on the breast of the American eagle, without any other supporters, to denote that the United States of America ought to rely on their own virtue.

"Reverse.—The pyramid signifies strength and duration. The eye over it, and the motto, allude to the many and signal interpositions of Providence in favor of the American cause. The date underneath is that of the Declaration of Independence; and the words under it signify the beginning of the new American era, which commences from that date."

In most of the above reports, a reference will be perceived to the devices and colors of the flag of the U. States, and many of the ideas presented in them are drawn from it, viz., the chief azure corresponding to the union of the flag, the pales corresponding to the stripes, which together constitute a whole; the constellation of stars also taken from the flag, and indicating a new State (composed of thirteen States) dependent upon their union. As these are the principal ideas presented in the arms of the United States, may we not reasonably conclude that, being borrowed from the flag, they are the views that prevailed at the time of its adoption, presented under another guise? The reference to eternity, in the arms, was indicated by the circle of stars in the flag; the reference to Providence, in the eye, was in the flag presented in the field of thirteen stripes, a combination of the red and white flags, which bore the mottoes: "*Qui transtulit sustinet*," and an "Appeal to Heaven."

It is intimated, in some of these reports, that the colors for the flag were adopted apart from other reasons, as implying certain virtues; of the fact of their implying them there can be no doubt, but that they were not immediately adopted into the flag for that reason, but rather because they were already in use, with these meanings attached to them, at least so far as the red and white colors were concerned, we think we have conclusively shown. We shall presently offer some suggestions relative to the blue color, which will indicate a more direct reason for its adoption than the virtues implied by it.

But to return to the account of the flag. We remarked, under the head of the Great Union Flag of the Colonies, that the stripes in the field of the flag were not only designed to show the union of the thirteen colonies, but also the number of members which composed it, and their dependence as a whole upon the Union. The first change in the flag of the United States, shows that this conclusion was a correct one. It was directed in the following resolution:—

> "*Be it enacted*, &c., That from and after the first day of May, Anno Domini one thousand seven hundred and ninety-five, the flag of the United States be fifteen stripes, alternate red and white. That the union be fifteen stars, white in a blue field." Approved January 13, 1794. (See Fig. 2, Plate III.)

This was the flag of the United States during the war of 1812-14.

In 1818, the flag of the United States was again altered, and, as we are informed, on the suggestion of the Hon. Mr. Wendover, of New York, a return was made to the thirteen stripes; as it was anticipated the flag would become unwieldy if a stripe was added on the admission of each State; and, moreover, by the plan proposed, the union of the old thirteen States, as well as the number of members composing the existing Union, would be presented by the flag of the United States. Mr. W. also proposed the arrangement of the stars in the union into the form of a single star. In this, there was a departure from the original design, as the perpetuity of the Union ceased to be indicated by the flag, as it had previously been in the circle of stars, except so far as indicated by the several stars forming one large star.

The Resolution of 1818 was as follows:-

> "*Be it enacted*, &c., That from and after the fourth day of July next, the flag of the United States be thirteen horizontal

stripes, alternate red and white; that the union be twenty stars, white, in a blue field.

"And, that, on the admission of a new State into the Union, one star be added to the union of the flag; and that such addition shall take effect on the fourth day of July next succeeding such admission." Approved April 4, 1818.

The flag planted on the National Palace of the city of Mexico had thirty stars in the union.

The following compliment was paid to this flag.

June 3, 1848, "Mr. Drayton submitted the following resolution; which was considered, by unanimous consent, and agreed to:—

"*Resolved*, That the Vice-President be requested to have the flag of the United States first erected by the American army upon the palace in the capital of Mexico, and now here presented, deposited for safe-keeping in the Department of State of the United States."—Page 370, Journal of the Senate 1847-48.

The union of the United States flag at present contains thirty-one stars. (See Fig. 3, Plate III.)

We have, in the preceding pages, offered many reasons for concluding that the devices in the flag, its colors, and the manner in which they were combined, originated in some circumstance directly connected with the history of the colonies, or in some practice which prevailed in the mother country. Particularly was this the case in the adoption of the emblem of union from the mother country. This leads us to make a few remarks as to the prominence given to the color blue in the reports on the adoption of the device for a Great Seal of the United States, and in its being the ground of the uniform of the United States. We have previously stated that its adoption was due to other circumstances directly, than its being typical of the virtues of perseverance, vigilance, and justice, though indirectly this meaning was involved in its adoption. First, blue was a favorite color in the colonies, as is proved by the fact of its being the uniform of the South Carolina troops in 1775. For we have seen that Colonel Moultrie caused a large blue flag to be made, with a crescent in one corner, to be uniform with the troops; and by the fact that the pine-tree flag of New England was a blue field, containing in the upper canton, next the staff, a St. George's cross on a white ground, and a pine-tree represented in the upper square formed by the cross. A reason for this color being a favorite in New England, may perhaps be found in the circumstance, that, in 1679, when the banner of the league and covenant was raised in Scotland, it was a red flag, the borders of which were edged with blue.[63] Borders of different color from the body of the flag, or from the shield of the coat of arms, are in heraldry, a common distinction, and as such was doubtless applied by the Covenanters (blue being the color of the field of the banner of Scotland, as we have seen), to indicate by whom this red flag was raised, and thus the blue color became identified with the league and covenant. After the defeat of Bothwell's Bridge, many of those people fled to the colonies, particularly to New England and New Jersey.

That feelings kindred to those excited among the Covenanters were aroused among the colonists, is shown by the mottoes on "the Union flag with a red field," already spoken of as displayed on a liberty-pole in New York city in 1775. Those mottoes were, "No Popery," and "George Rex and the liberties of America." It was probably in reference to his being commander of the armies of the colonies, united in a solemn league and covenant in defence of civil and religious liberty, that General Washington adopted as his badge a light blue riband, which had already been identified with a similar league and covenant in Scotland. At a later day, on the adoption of an Union flag as the flag of the United Colonies, the color of the field of the union (derived, as was the blue border of the red flag of the Covenanters, from the banner of Scotland) being blue, this color became identified with that which gave nationality to the colonies, viz., their union, and on this account was adopted as the ground of the national uniform, and as the color for the chief or union, both in the arms of the United States and in their flag.

That the prevailing colors of the uniforms of the army at that time corresponded to the colors of the flag, is a well-known fact. Thus the facings of the blue coats were red, the color of the plumes white, tipped with red, &c. The buff and blue, commonly regarded as the continental uniform, was that of the general officers, and not of the body of the troops. In the navy, the same was the case. The prevailing colors of the uniform of the officers of the navy were blue and red; those of the uniform of the marine officers, green and white: the colors of the flag of the United States, and of the flag of the floating batteries, before given, viz., white, with a green tree in the middle, &c. &c.

That such considerations operate in the selection of colors for uniforms, is proved by the fact that the uniform of the United States corps of cadets, a corps instituted and kept up with a view to foster and preserve military knowledge in our country, instead of being of the national color, blue, is gray trimmed with black. This color for the uniform of that corps was chosen in 1815, out of compliment to the services of the brigade commanded by General Scott at Chippewa, &c., in the war of 1812-14. The embargo and the war having cut off the supply of blue cloths, the commissary-general of purchases was forced temporarily to supply that brigade with a substitute of gray, trimmed with black.

As this, then, was the origin of the color of the uniform of the corps of cadets, may we not conclude that, for the reasons assigned, blue was adopted as our national color, out of compliment to the Union, with which, as we have shown, it was intimately connected.

Having given the preceding account of our National Flag, we now add the names of those connected with its different phases.

1st. General Washington.

2d. Benjamin Franklin, Mr. Lynch, and Mr. Harrison; the Committee of Conference, with General Washington, on the organization of the army, of which Colonel Joseph Reed was Secretary.

3d. The Marine Committee; Mr. Bartlett, Mr. Hancock, Mr. Hopkins, Mr. Deane, Mr. Lewis, Mr. Crane, Mr. R. Morris, Mr. Read, Mr. Chase, Mr. R. H. Lee, Mr. Hewes, Mr. Gadsden, and Mr. Houston.

4th. The Board of War; Mr. J. Adams, Mr. Sherman, Mr. Harrison, Mr. Wilson, and Mr. E. Rutledge.

With this array of names before us, of those who, with others, established our liberty and Union, and the idea we have developed, that the devices adopted by them for the National Ensign of our country were intended to intimate the perpetuity of that country's union, may we not truly say of Washington and his compeers, now resting in their graves, as connected with those devices, There is neither speech nor language, but their voices are heard among them. Their sound has gone out into all lands, and their words into the ends of the world, proclaiming their trust in Providence, that that Union should only perish, when the sun and moon shall be darkened, and the stars shall withdraw their light.

Footnotes

[1] "Standards, somewhat similar to those represented on the Assyrian bas-reliefs, were in use in Egypt. Some sacred animal or emblem was also generally placed upon them."

[2] Siege of Boston, Frothingham, p. 104, *note*.

[3] American Archives, 4th series, vol. ii. p. 863.

[4] Ibid. p. 1582.

[5] General Putnam was named *Israel*.

[6] American Archives, 4th series, vol. ii. p. 1687.

[7] The General's tent.

[8] Adams's Roman Antiquities, p. 322.

[9] American Archives, 4th series, vol. iv. p. 711.

[10] Holmes's Annals, vol. ii. p. 227.

[11] Brande's Dictionary of Literature, &c. *Crescent.*

[12] American Archives, 4th series, vol. iii. p. 1126.

[13] Ibid. vol. iv. p. 570.

[14] American Archives, 4th series, vol. v. p. 568.

[15] Ibid. vol. v. p. 1299.

[16] Journal of Congress, vol. ii. p. 165.

[17] Boston Gazette and Country Journal, Sept. 15, 1777.

[18] Parker. Terms used in British Heraldry, p. 40.

[19] Parker. Terms used in British Heraldry, p. 148.

[20] Ibid. p. 149.

[21] Parker. Terms used in British Heraldry, p. 42.

[22] Ibid. p. 273.

[23] Ibid. p. 9.

[24] Parker. Terms used in British Heraldry, p. 315.

[25] Note by Author.—This white edging would, however, show the union of the two flags, which otherwise might not have been apparent. We are told, in De Foe's History of the Union, that great jealousy for the ancient banners of their respective kingdoms, was shown both by Scots and English.

[26] Parker. Terms used in British Heraldry, pp. 315-16.

[27] Parker. Terms used in British Heraldry, pp. 315-16.

[28] Winthrop's New England, vol. i. p. 146.

[29] Ibid. vol. i. pp. 155-6.

[30] Ibid. vol. i. pp. 158.

[31] Winthrop's New England, vol. i. p. 158.

[32] Winthrop's New England, vol. i. p. 158.

[33] Ibid. vol. i. p. 180.

[34] Winthrop's New England, vol. i. p. 187.

[35] Winthrop's New England, vol. ii. p. 344.

[36] Hazard, vol. i. p. 554.

[37] History of the Union of Scotland and England, by Danl. De Foe, p. 528.

[38] The Boston News Letter, No. 197, from Monday, Jan. 19, to Monday, Jan. 26, 1707.

[39] Neal's History of New England, p. 585.

[40] Siege of Boston, p. 104, note.

[41] T. Westcott, Notes and Queries. Literary World, Oct. 2, 1852.

[42] American Archives, 4th series, vol. iv. p. 467.

[43] Siege of Boston, p. 283.

[44] American Archives, 4th series, vol. iv. p. 711.

[45] British Annual Register, 1776, p. 147.

[46] King's Regulations for the British Army, Colors, &c.

[47] American Archives, 4th series, vol. v. p. 423.

[48] From this, we may justly conclude that the Committee of Conference, composed of Dr. Franklin, Mr. Lynch, and Mr. Harrison, had the subject of the flag under consideration, and that the flag prepared under their supervision was the one displayed as the flag of the United Colonies, on the day the army organized by them, General Washington, &c., went into being.

[49] Siege of Boston, p. 261.

[50] Mass. Historical Collections, 2d series, vol. ii. p. 228.

[51] American Archives, 4th series, vol. iv. p. 1179.

[52] American Archives, 4th series, vol. iv. p. 965.

[53] Ibid. vol. v. p. 823.

[54] American Archives, 4th series, vol. ii. p. 1582.

[55] American Archives, 4th series, vol. ii. p. 1662.

[56] American Archives, 4th series, vol. ii. p. 1738.

[57] American Archives, 4th series, vol. v. p. 568. South Carolina Provincial Congress.

[58] Franklin's Works, vol. iii. p. 25.

[59] Frothingham's Siege of Boston.

[60] "As the pales or pallets consist of an uneven number, they ought in strictness to be blazoned — Argt. 6 pallets gules; but as the thirteen pieces allude to the thirteen States, they are blazoned according to the number of *pieces paleways*."

[61] The pen is run through the words, "with thirteen strings," in the original.

[62] "In the arms of Scotland, as manifested in the royal atchievement, the double fressure which surrounds the lion is borne *flory* and *counter-flory* (with *fleurs-de-lis*), which is in consequence of a treaty that was entered into between Charlemagne, then Emperor and King of France, and Achius, King of Scotland; to denote that the French lilies should guard and defend the Scottish lion."

[63] Walter Scott's Old Mortality, vol. ii. p. 116.